Ghost Stories
& Legends of
Prince Edward Island

Julie V. Watson
Photographs
by John C. Watson

Ghost Stories & Legends of Prince Edward Island

Copyright © 1988 by Julie V. Watson

Hounslow Press
A member of the Dundurn Group

Publisher: Anthony Hawke
Designer: Gerard Williams
Composition: Accurate Typesetting Limited
Printer: Transcontinental Printing Inc.

Publication was assisted by the **Canada Council**, the **Book Publishing Industry Development Program** of the **Department of Canadian Heritage**, the **Ontario Arts Council**, and the **Ontario Publishing Centre** of the **Ministry of Culture, Tourism and Recreation.**

Care has been taken to trace the ownership of copyright material used in this book. The author and the publisher welcome any information enabling them to rectify any reference or credit in subsequent editions.

Fourth Printing: March 1995
Fifth Printing: March 1998

Printed and bound in Canada

Hounslow Press
8 Market Street
Suite 200
Toronto, Ontario, Canada
M5E 1M6

Hounslow Press
73 Lime Walk
Headington, Oxford
England
OX3 7AD

Hounslow Press
250 Sonwil Drive
Buffalo, NY
U.S.A. 14225

Contents

Introduction   1
The Beginning   2
An Early History   6
The Creation of the World   11
    Minegoo's Creation   12
    Glooscap   14
    Girl Fish   14
    Globe-Trotter   15
    Storm King   16
    Origin of Flies   17
The Origin of the Melicites   19
The Fair Miniota   22
La Belle Marie: Burned at the Stake   27
Miminegash   31
    He Who Walks the Lights of the Northern Sky   31
    Refugee's Revenge   33
The Phantom Ship of Northumberland Strait   35
    Sea Cannon of the Strait   38
    Explanation   39
The Great Seal Robbery   41
A Pirate, Island Born   46
    Second Sight Sally Sees Doom for *Snowdrift*   47
    Winter — Kills *Snow Squall*   48
Buried Treasure   49
    Kidd Holds to Agreement — No Human Sacrifice,
    No Treasure   50

DeRoma's Gold 52
Blue's Cove Treasure 54
West Point 55
Dig in the Dark of the Moon 55
Cape Le Force 61
The Murder of Abel 66
Abel's Cape 71
Lost Baby Lures Ghost Again and Again 78
The Shadow of Holland Cove 82
The Fork in the Graveyard 85
Sea Serpents and Monsters 88
West Point 88
Little Pond 89
Miminegash 89
Romantic Link Made on Hallowe'en 91
The Ghost of Barlow Road 94
Naked Nathan 96
Fairy Rings 97
Tignish 98
Ghost of St. Simon and St. Jude 98
Haw Bush Treasure 99
Chest on a Reef a Lure to the Phantom Ship? 101
Blumphey's Ghost at Tignish Run 101
The Ghostly Miller of Clyde River 105
The Smugglers of Holland Cove 108
A Phenomenon of a Battle at Sea 118
Forerunners 122
The Phantom Train 123
The Phantom Bell Ringers: A Story of the
Auld Kirk of St. James 124
Loss of the *Fairy Queen* 131
The Yankee Gale 135
Crossing at the Capes in Winter 143
Horse Through the Ice 147
Dead Man's Pond 151
Treacherous Travel 153
Slightly Siberian Souris 155

Fly Boys' Hero   158
Tea Hill Disaster   160
Phantom Submarine Among the Evidence of a War
    that Came Too Close   163
Great Humming Bird of the Sky   166
    "Bye Now"   169
They Made 'Em Tough   171
Nigger — The Dog That Would Not Die   173
The Bulldog and the Bear   176

Acknowledgements

I would like to thank the following people and institutions who gave me much valuable help and advice in the preparation of this book: *Carol Livingstone* of West Point, P.E.I.; *David Weale* of The University of Prince Edward Island and my Folklore course classmates; *The Public Archives of Prince Edward Island*; and *The Prince Edward Island Heritage Foundation*.

Introduction

I t has been said far too many times and, as it happens, untruthfully, that Prince Edward Island, even Canada, has a dull history — a past with little romance and adventure and an unimaginative acceptance of law and order that provide scant material for the story-teller.

Allow me to go on record as saying that is strictly untrue. The difference, I think, is that being settled by peoples with high moral standards, and a desire to present themselves and their communities in the best light, meant that many of the more lurid deeds and peoples were simply not widely discussed.

Add to that an almost non-existent communication system and you have mystery — the very foundation of the legends of today.

The citizenry of the province certainly do have a wealth of legends and true tales that are as exciting as fiction. In researching this book, I found many facts that amazed me. For instance, the fact that Flat Nose George Curry was a member of the gang led by Sundance Kid and Butch Cassidy that plagued the wild west in the 1890s — until a posse put an end to his career of crime around 1900. This is particularly amazing as our neighbours in Riverdale are Currys — descendants I wonder?

The Beginning

March 16th, 1987 — the day I began writing the book which I shall, for the sake of space, simply call *Legends*. It stands out in my mind because it was the day the St. Patrick's storm hit, leaving me alone in a house surrounded by huge drifts of snow, for three days.

St. Pat's storm had arrived a day early that year, not because Mother Nature miscalculated, but rather because a longer stay was planned for the annual visitation.

In my case, it was a blessing in disguise. My husband, Jack, was up and out by 6:00 a.m. As a mechanic for the National Park, responsible for clearing their own roads, he was concerned because the grader was in pieces in the garage and he was the only one available to reassemble it; so off he went, driving the thirty-two miles to work in the early stages of the storm. He decided, just after arriving, that probably he would not make it home until conditions improved. And he didn't.

So there I was, alone except for Penny, our Border Collie, who was about to set a new record for "holding it." It was a deceptive day, not looking all that bad from my office window. But the snow which eventually drifted up and right over the back door was evidence of just how much white stuff was coming down.

At four o'clock I bravely filled a water bucket, bundled myself up in scarf, woolly hat, gloves, and two pairs of slacks, and braved the elements to head for the barn. It was tricky. The snow had drifted about fifteen feet high between house and barn. For weeks now we had been trecking up and over it, but new drifts on top of the old made finding sure footing difficult. This particular winter the wind had been blowing the snow so that drifts encircled the house and barn. At times it was like living in a pit, the one around the barn dropped off suddenly and must have been about nine — or maybe ten — feet down to the ground. I knew it was higher than I could reach, even standing on my tiptoes and stretching to my fingertips.

I managed to manoeuvre the bucket down by driving my toes in and sort of descending the drift like a mountain climber. Next Christmas I think I'd like some of those pointy steel things climbers strap on their toes to help in climbing vertical faces.

Of course, that was not the end of it. The sleet had frozen the door shut so I had to chop the ice off to get into the barn. When I wrenched the door open and stepped in, I darn near spilled all the water as I fell into another snowdrift — this one inside the barn!

Not deep, but enough to startle the unwary. Cursing at broken heat cables that let the water freeze, I gave the pregnant mare the half bucket of water that had survived the trip and threw in an extra flake of hay.

Don't feel sorry for her! She was snug and warm in spite of the snow which had filtered through every crack around the door. Freshly bedded with deep straw and lots to eat, I envied her. I was the fool who had to venture back across the drift — this time facing into the wind.

Obviously I made it. In fact I even took time out to walk over to the drive to measure the snow in the driveway against myself — to see how deep it was. Considering my own height of five feet, it was about five feet, eight inches deep, less than twelve hours into the storm.

This brings me back to why the storm was a good thing in my life.

For some reason, being alone in a house battered by storms, brings out some creative force. The need to write becomes intense, and I have few distractions — no one to spend a pleasant hour with, to prepare meals for, or to clean up after. I have no reason to go to bed until I'm ready. Indeed, it seemed senseless to rush to bed since the only incentive to getting up in the morning was yet another trip to the barn. (When that time came, I had the misfortune to miss my step and fall down the nine foot drop, not only spilling the water and bruising my behind, but also doing great harm to my dignity.)

The snow continued to fall, to blow, and to sculpt new obstacles in my life. A CBC news commentator summed it up, saying, "It's white Prince Edward Island will be wearin' for St. Paddy's Day."

My reason for recording this event is the awareness that developed within me as I waited out the storm.

In the normal total comfort of a heated house with a stove to cook on and television and books to entertain, not to mention the cupboards and freezer full of food, a companion to share the unexpected holiday, and the inevitable visits of ploughs to release us from the snowbound prison, it was hard to envision life as it was in the days when most legends and folklore of the Island began.

But finding myself alone in a house that creaks and groans in the wind, and being forced to rely on candles and a woodstove when the power failed, really set the mood. How, I wonder, could those early residents have survived in primitive housing, where they were trapped until a thaw cleared the path to supplies and human contact? Without the ability of women to cook wonderful sustaining meals from meagre supplies brought in after hours of laborious hunting or bone-chilling work by their men, and without the talents of the story-tellers to entertain, life would have been bleak indeed.

The Paddy's Day storm heightened my perspective to a point that I can only hope readers will be able to duplicate, when reading some of the tales of the past. If they seem untrue, or exaggerated beyond realism, take into account the conditions and circumstances in which they were born.

An Early History

To appreciate fully any tales of early prince Edward Island, it is best to understand at least a little about the early peoples and how they lived. For it is with these early dwellers and the circumstances of their lives that most of the legends, folklore, and true tales (as strange as any fiction imaginable), began.

To comprehend truly the people and the tales about them, you must understand that settlement was not easy. Most of the people were poor and unskilled. The general population had little education, with the exception of members of the government or high-ranking military officers.

While trying to eke out existence from a harsh land, they were beset by pirates, privateers, enemy forces, plagues of mice, devastating fires, and, at times, corrupt landlords and agents. Their very lives were threatened by the wars of other nations: the French, the British, the American Revolution in the early days, then the great wars of the twentieth century. The expulsion of the Acadians was reflected years later by the arrival of the Loyalists, fleeing from their own intolerable situation. Although an Island, the influence of the outside world was never far away.

A short history will provide insight into the province's development, but bear in mind that while these facts were being established, all of the aforementioned obstacles and many more were affecting the lives of the individual.

The earliest known residents were Micmac Indians, a proud and ferocious race, who, some believe, used the Island only as a summer camping ground. It is with the Micmac that many of our finest legends begin.

In fact, the Micmac account for the very creation of the land that makes up our Island home will be found in "Minegoo's Creation." It is believed that in the years just prior to settlement by Europeans (white men), there were three to four thousand Micmac living on or near the Island.

In 1534, their way of life was to change. Jacques Cartier sighted, landed on, and duly reported to his ruler, the existence of the fairest land one could hope to find. Over the next hundred years the most frequent white visitors were French and Basque fishermen. In fact, it was not until the second decade of the eighteenth century, in 1720, that Europeans began to settle permanently in any numbers.

At that time the Island was heavily wooded. Because of this, the first settlement, primarily by the French, was along the shores, and it required much hard labour even to clear enough land to build a home, let alone fields for crops. For a great number of years, settlement didn't extend more than one farm deep from the shoreline. Travel was by canoe, making the development of roads a slow process. The Hillsborough River was the main water route, accounting for the distribution of the settlers.

Early settlement concentrated around Charlottetown Harbour, particularly at Port La Joie, up the Hillsborough River, and in St. Peters, as well as in the areas of Tracadie, Orwell, and South Lake. In St. Peters, where the main settlement took place until the 1740s, during those first two decades the white population numbered between 300 and 450 persons.

Generally, the North Shore area was slow to be settled, because sand dunes and shallow waters barring the entrances to the bays and rivers made it difficult to bring the large ships in to shore.

This problem continues even today, resulting in all large shipping taking place from the south shore, and even the small fishing boats still facing problems getting in and out of harbour safely.

Gradually, through the 1740s and 50s, population increased along the north shore, particularly between Malpeque and Savage Harbour. In this era, the 1750s, the French were expelled from the Fundy area by the British and many came to the Island, creating a refugee camp as much as a colony, increasing the population to almost 3,000.

The Island remained under French rule until 1758 when the British, having taken Fort Louisbourg for the second and final time, rounded up the French settlers on the Island and deported them. This expulsion and its consequences mark a shameful part of history. Only about 300 Acadians remained, located south of Malpeque Bay, and around Rustico and Souris.

In 1763, the Island was formally awarded to the British Crown. There was pressure on the Crown to award land to influential petitioners; thus, in 1764, Samuel Holland came to survey the Island. It was divided into sixty-six townships or "lots," each supposed to contain 20,000 acres: one small lot, nominally of 6,000 acres, and three town-sites with attached "royalties," one in each county.

By 1767 Holland had done his job, and the British Board of Commissioners conducted a lottery in which the townships were awarded to petitioners. Each new proprietor had to agree to pay quit-rents to the Crown, and to settle his lot with 100 Protestant, non-British persons within ten years.

Unfortunately for the Crown and the early settlers, most proprietors were not particularly interested in their acquisitions or in fulfilling the requirements. Lots changed hands; rents went unpaid; and a land-ownership problem began that would trouble the Island until after Confederation — still almost a century away.

Basic settlement patterns followed those of the French, a natural progression, as the first British simply took over what had been begun by the French.

A few of the proprietors tried to settle their lots, and by 1800 some communities were developing. The Tracadie Bay area was among the more notable, where Captain John MacDonald of Glenalladale brought several hundred Scottish Highlanders in to farm the area between 1770 and 1775. He did not stick strictly to the letter of the agreement, however, as the Scots were Roman Catholic.

The eastern shores of Malpeque Bay were settled by Protestant Scottish Lowlanders. Lowland Scots and English Protestants settled the New London area, and a number of Protestant families set down roots in the Covehead area. Rustico was still French. The religious patterns continued for many years; in fact they can still be seen today by the careful observer.

This influx brought most of the northshore land under cultivation, and established transportation patterns that ran primarily east and west. The main route from North to South shores was still the mighty Hillsborough River, and it was here and across the bays of the North Shore, that the first ferries operated.

Roads were developed slowly with the first of note connecting Charlottetown to Malpeque and St. Peters. By 1850 a basic road network was in place with roads running north and south to link into these principal routes. Settlement naturally followed the creation of the roads, and the population crept southward.

Beginning in the 1840s, relatively large numbers of Irish Roman Catholics immigrated and tended to concentrate their settlements inland in areas like St. Anne's and Hope River.

The Island had been granted separate government from Nova Scotia in 1769 on the presumption that government would be financed by the quit rents due from proprietors. As they evaded these responsibilities, land ownership became a volatile issue for the populace, recorded by the first census in 1798 as numbering 4,372.

Immigration continued, and by 1891 the population had

grown to 109,000 before it began a decline which reached a low of about 88,000 in the 1930s. Today's population is not much more than 15,000 above that of 1891.

During the first half of the nineteenth century, many residents were able to acquire title to their lands, so that by Confederation about fifty per cent of the lots were in freehold tenure. After Confederation the provincial government was able to purchase land, and turn it over to tenants by lease purchase agreements.

The primary source of insecurity, and all too often dishonest dealings, was gone, and the population settled to a pattern of development and modernization following that of Canada as a whole. Modern shipping, stronger governments and law enforcement, electricity, the railroad, the automobile — all manner of things — served to change life, to move it along, just as the pattern continues today.

The
Creation of the World

T he Micmac legend of the creation of the world is slightly different from that of other tribes, and yet is substantially the same. They believed that at first the globe was one vast and entire ocean, inhabited by no creature except a mighty bird, whose eyes were fire and whose glances were lightning; and the clapping of whose wings was thunder.

On the bird's descent to the ocean, and on his approaching it, a canoe instantly rose to the surface, upon which was seated Glooscap and a woman. These two persons were surrounded by all kinds of animals, and a discussion was held as to the matter that must underlie the water. Four animals were sent down to find out this substance, three of which failed; the last, a musk-rat, returned with some mud in his forepaw. This, the woman scraped off, and began to work around in her hands. It grew rapidly and then was placed in the water, where it continued to increase in size.

The wolf began to be troublesome, and the woman, becoming angry with him, scolded him, and finally threw him upon the island. He ran around the outside, making in the plastic soil indentations with his paws, and causing the shores of the rivers to be harder than any other soil. Herbs and trees began to grow, and a small shrub planted by the woman grew until it reached the sky. Overhead a beautiful object was seen which fascinated the dwellers on the island. The woman sent the man up the tree to find out what it was.

It looked like an old woman, and he caught it with a snare. The woman below became very angry, and several animals were asked to go up. The racoon went up, but in the heat was scorched and fell down. The mole ascended, and when the heat increased, burrowed and cut the snare, allowing the sun to go on its course, but in so doing had his nose scorched; and it remains so till this day.

Minegoo's Creation

The Great Spirit, the creator of the earth and everything to be found under the sun, had finished his most creative work, forming a universe. But he found he still had a goodly lump of red clay.

Standing in his heavenly workshop, pondering what to do with it, he noticed the clay was the colour of his people. Fingering the magical material, he found it had formed a crescent shape, perfect, he realized, to create an island which would be the fairest to be found on earth.

The Great Spirit's creation was so beautiful he called it Minegoo, and decided to keep it at his heavenly workshop so that he could use it himself up among the stars.

Yet, the Great Spirit is a kindly being, and felt wrong in keeping such a wonderful place from the earth.

Story-tellers describe how the Great Spirit lifted Minegoo to his strong shoulders on a beautiful June day, opening the portals of heaven, and flying to the place of Laughing Waters, where He gently nestled the Island in the protective curve created by the mainland. These waters are, of course, known today as the Gulf of St. Lawrence.

It was as he knew it would be. Minegoo settled into the Laughing Waters like a beautiful jewel, an emerald which grew greater in its beauty and tranquillity as the days passed.

Minegoo came to hold a special place in the Great Spirit's heart. The more he flew around it, the more often he visited, the more pleased he was with his creation.

It became a place of refuge from the wearying business of being a god. He rested here for days at a time, savouring the luscious woods, emerald meadows, and golden shores. Whispering breezes brought bird song to his ears and carried the gentle lullaby of sea winds and waves to gentle his soul. The great blankets of winter snow held their own special beauty and renewed the earth.

Minegoo captivated the Great Spirit. He began to spend so much time in the paradise he had created that he almost forgot his duties, and even his real home, particularly during the summers. In fact this situation continued as centuries came and went. He would laze away the summers in serene solitude.

But finally he realized that to keep this perfect place from others was wrong. It was thinking of his people, the red men, that had caused him to create Minegoo. Now he was keeping the earth paradise for his own selfish use. And so he decided to limit his visits to one each summer and, more important, to share Minegoo with his brethren.

Soon the first Indian paddled across the Strait, discovering a land so impressive, he returned and brought others of his tribe to enjoy the summer camping ground. A tradition was begun then that continues even until today, when thousands still visit the shores during the summer to enjoy the gentle breezes, emerald fields, sapphire skies and wonderful solitude.

So great has been the love of many of these peoples that they can never bear to depart from the shores of the great Island of Minegoo. Rather they stay through the season when the great blanket of snow still covers the red clay soil; the snow moistens and protects the ground and its life, until the warm sun rises high in the sky to announce the coming of spring.

Glooscap

One of the greatest Micmac legendary figures is Glooscap whose attributes are a strange combination of the human and the divine — with omnipotent power — which he exerted in providing human aid on a large scale.

The tradition respecting Glooscap states that he came to this country from the East — far across the great sea; when he went away, he went toward the West; and there he is still. When he arrived, he had a woman with him, whom he addressed as Noogumich (grandmother); she was not his wife; he was never known to have had one; what became of her is a mystery, as traditions fail to reveal her going from Micmac legend.

At the motion of his magic wand, the moose and cariboo, the bear and lucifee, hastened to his hand. The elements were also under his control. When his enemies assembled, numerous as the leaves of the forest, he mysteriously extinguished their fires, intensifying the cold to such a degree that in the morning the hostile host lay dead. But Glooscap was benevolent; wanderers were made welcome at his great wigwam where he entertained them right royally.

Girl Fish

Glooscap on one occasion put out to sea in his canoe, which was made of granite rock; he took as a passenger a young woman; she proved to be a bad girl — and this was evident by the troubles that ensued. A storm arose and the waves dashed over the canoe; he accused her of being the cause through her evil deeds, and so he determined to rid himself of her. He stood in for the land, leaped ashore, but would not allow her to follow, pushing the canoe off again with the girl in it and telling her to become whatever she desired to be. She was transformed into a great fish, said to have a huge dorsal fin like the sail of a boat.

Glooscap did not stay once the whites came. Offended at their treachery, he decided to go away to the west to live. He made his wish known, and a whale came, asking what he could do. Glooscap, calling the whale Grandfather, asked to be taken across the waters to the magical land in the west. In thanks for carrying him on his back for such a distance, Glooscap gave the whale a pipe, filled with tobacco and lighted. The whale, puffing away on the pipe, left Glooscap high on a hill to make his new home.

The Micmacs sometimes visited Glooscap in his spacious wigwam in the beautiful land in the west. The journey was long and difficult, crossing a mountain, ascending a perpendicular bluff, and descending over a hump that left them hanging free in the air. Two huge serpents which darted out their tongues to destroy all passers-by had to be passed; then a wall circling the land, negotiated. Not a simple task of scaling, for this wall was of thick, heavy cloud which rose and fell at intervals, and struck the ground so hard that whoever was caught underneath would be crushed. The good, however, could dart under unscathed and would find themselves in the beautiful region Glooscap now called home.

He had taught them, when he was with them, that there was such a place and, if good in life, they would go with him at death.

Globe-Trotter

The original globe-trotter was a Micmac who went around the world in four minutes — a record to date! As vanity was to be avoided, the brave was careful not to show off his talents, keeping one leg tied up to prevent his running too swiftly. Only when called upon to traverse the earth did he remove the thong, speeding off in one direction and returning from the other, proving that he had been around the world.

Storm King

A certain Indian family which lived on the Island shore maintained itself principally by fishing. Their favourite food was eels. At one time, however, the wind blew so fiercely that they could not fish, so they walked along the shore to look for any fish that might have drifted in with the tide. In a short time they reached Rocky Point. Here a ledge of rocks extended out into the Strait. On the most distant rock sat a large bird, the Storm King, flapping its wings and by this means causing winds.

The Indians decided to fool the Storm King into stopping the winds. Convincing him by trickery that he was cold, they offered to carry him to shore on their backs. One man purposely stumbled, causing the Storm King's wing to be broken. The Indians bound the wing, advising the great bird to keep it quiet until it healed.

Calm came over the land and the waters while the wing healed. But soon that very calm caused devastation. The waters became covered by a scum that prevented eel fishing as effectively as had the rough waters. Again the Indians turned to the Storm King and found that the wing was partially healed. They advised him to keep both wings flapping steadily but gently, so as not to cause more damage. A gentle ripple topped the water, breezes cooled the land.

And still the foolish braves were not satisfied. When they hunted whales, none would appear, so again they turned to mischievous pursuits.

Approaching a great city of the white man, a city ruled over by a king, they dosed the sentries, passed seven enclosures, and eventually came to the palace and invaded the room of the king's daughter. Even this prey eluded them, for the princess screamed causing much excitement, even the firing of the defensive cannon. The Indians fled — presumably returning to the pursuit of eel fishing.

Origin of Flies

It is said that the Micmac has an explanation for every-thing in life. Sometimes these seem strange or without logical reasoning, but even so they are delightful.

One day two brothers were with their father in his wigwam when he fell into a deep sleep. The two brothers silently set fire to a pile of birch bark, then crept out, sealing the door behind them. The flames quickly rose up and consumed the wigwam. The brothers ignored the screams of their father, walking away from the scene and leaving him to his fate.

Later they returned, gathering up the ashes that were all that remained of their father. These were pounded out to a powder, then held up and blown into the wind with instructions to become flies. Of course they did, and it is from these that all flies of all types descended.

The
Origin of the Melicites

This tradition of the Prince Edward Island Micmacs was put into print by one Lawrence W. Watson in 1899. He said it came from Lennox Island Indian Reserve, with weighty evidence that it was true.

"Long before the French had come, while still the Micmac was the only monarch in fair Epagweit, "resting on the wave," — he and the wild beasts against which he strove — the Indians had come together for a pow-wow and for feasting on the bank above the "bold, steep, sandy shore" of Caskamkek" (known as Cascumpec today). And as they feasted here, two dogs, the petted hunting companions of as many stalwart braves, first snarling over the bone each hungered after, then maddened into fury, for that neither could secure the tempting feast already tasted of, fell into savage struggle, and rent the air with howls of rage and pain.

The Indians, with the keenness of their hunger satisfied, hastened to the scene, some in curious mood or speculative, some delighting in the varying fortunes of the struggling beasts. And first of those to reach the spot was he who owned the dog which at that time appeared to be the weaker of the two. In pity for his canine friend, in angry humiliation at his sad defeat, he struck the other hound a staggering, savage blow, whereupon the owner of the stronger dog remonstrated, saying "Let them alone; leave them to fight till the stronger wins; he risks his life who strikes a friend of mine." To whom the other answered: "You and your dog are one," and dealt him, all unguarded, a swift and heavy blow. The smitten athlete, quick upon his feet, closed upon the other, and a mighty struggle then began.

Each warrior had his followers and his friends, who praising now his tactics or his skill, now shouting taunt and challenge to his panting antagonists, gradually stirred up those around them into sympathy and support, until one side slowly weakened, driven inch by inch towards the woods, and the plain was strewn with dying braves and dead.

Victory gave the vanquishers strength as they pushed the weaker, disordered band far into the lengthening shadows of the thick spruce wood. Like hunted deer the fugitives fled, until at last, worn out by battle and retreat, they halted, taking council as to how they should proceed.

It was determined to reach, if possible, and to follow an old footpath leading to the south, as the victors, having rested would, no doubt, hasten by the newer, wider trail to where the bark canoes were beached and made secure by strips of hide to stakes fast driven in the sand. Fear furnished strength; the fugitives hurried on — slow through the thicket, swift in the pathway, southward and seaward, on to the shore.

To embark was the work of a very few minutes, when out from the land shot the birch-bark canoes, swift as the arrow from the bow. Well did the fugitives know the strength of the arms which would speed the light craft to the eluded pursuers.

On, on they sped, on to the east, past where the sea-cow herded in Buslooakade (Cape Traverse), on to the inlet which still tells the story, for men call it yet by the name Canoe Cove. Here disembarking, they made a portage northwards to a river flowing from the west (West or

"Elliot" River), down which they paddled, passing on the left the point of land on which Charlottetown now stands. Still further onward, over the course of the sister stream flowing from the north-east, on to its head, where a second portage brought the weary ones to the north shore again near Boogoosumkek, as the Indians later named St. Peter's Bay. Thence, skirting the shore towards the rising sun, the voyagers continued till they rounded what the white man now calls East Cape, whence, setting out to sea, they made for the mainland, Cape Breton Island, (Oonamagik), and landed at Weukuch, "the place of red ochre," (in Mic-mac "Boosaal.") Here they first dwelt, but in process of time increasing in number they spread to the south into many new stations.

Yet so sore their defeat, so deep-rooted their fear, they changed their speech in such a way that the Mic-mac could not understand them when they spoke. And they taught their little ones to dread the coming of the Mic-mac and to answer when a stranger questioned only this — "I do not understand." In after years some Mic-macs, more daring than their fellows, crossed the Straight of Northumberland to the mainland on the south, whence returning home they brought the curious tale of how they there had seen a race of men, in face and customs as themselves, but understanding not their language. "For," said they, "to every question which we asked they answered nothing more than this — I do not understand you."

But the old men dreamed at night of mighty battle and of hot pursuit of erstwhile friendly kinsmen fleeing eastward till they passed from sight before they reached the point "where the current flows close in by the shore" at Weje-witk (Margaree in Cape Breton).

And because the language of this tribe seemed to them a confusion of the Mic-mac tongue, the great Wabanaki race of Indians coming later from the west, gave to the strange band the name of MELICITES, which in their language signifies, "a broken or corrupted speech."

The Fair Miniota

This accounting of the Micmac legend about Miniota was published by J. Edward Rendle in 1898 in The Prince Edward Island Magazine.

"Long years before the advent of the white man upon the Island, the province was traversed by the trails of the red men. Through the forest primeval they found their way to their destination, unaided by blazed tree, mound or stone; trusting all to their keen eye. The rivers were the highways for those who travelled by canoe, and many scenes, strange and sad were enacted on our waters. Those Indian highways constituted a singular network over our Island, and many braves started from their campfires and lodges who were destined never to return.

"If these scenes of former years could be revived what strange emotions would thrill our hearts? The Micmacs have nearly all gone from us, and much of their history has died with them. Their arrows are broken, their wigwams are dust. Their council-fire has long since gone out, and their war-cry is fast receding to the untrodden West. Slowly but surely they climb the distant mountains, and read their doom in the setting sun.

"So soliloquised Ralph Thompson, as he stood one summer morning in the year 18--, on the summit of one of the high banks at the entrance to Charlottetown Harbour, in the vicinity of the old French Fort. He was that morning "monarch of all he surveyed;" or at least he thought so. In front of him lay the still and placid bay, and all around him the almost unbroken forest. His mood left him perfectly unconscious of where he went; he had entered a path, admiring the scenery, but not thinking where it led, or what place he sought, when a huge stump, or gnarled root suddenly appeared before him and awoke him from his trance.

"Outlet there was none. All around him towered stately pines, their tops reaching as it seemed to the skies. The path was so winding that, as he looked round amazed, he could not even imagine how he came there. To go back seemed quite as difficult as to proceed. There was but one way, and that was to climb over it. This he did, and found the beaten track before him. Following the path brought him to a small creek running out into the harbour. Stopping here to rest, he discovered by its side a conical-shaped stone of a peculiar colour, and weighing about 30 pounds. A circle was made in the earth around it, and in it there lay maize and Indian ornaments of various kinds. Thinking he had found a curiosity relating to the Indians, he attempted to collect the ornaments and remove the stone, but had hardly grasped it when his attention was called to two Indians, a little further up the stream, who were going through some kind of gestations to attract his notice. As they drew near to him, and passing the stone, they laid some bunches of berries inside the circle surrounding it, and entered into conversation with him.

"To the Indian, the material world is sentient and intelligent. Birds, beasts, and stones have ears for human prayers, and are endued with an influence on human destiny. The stone that he had found was one of the famous Micmac "medicine stones." and was held by the two Indians in great reverence, and on asking the oldest of them concerning it, he related to him the legend of the Fair Miniota.

"A great many moons ago, a great Souriquois chief named Kiotsaton, who was a great warrior, and had come from Oonamagik (the name Cape Breton is known by to the Micmacs), dwelt for a time with his brethren on the Island of St. John. During his stay among them, he at one time fixed his wigwam near this stream, Minnewauken — mysterious water as it was called by the Indians, (and which by 1898 was a small creek lying to the N.W. of the old French Fort and flowing into Warren Farm Cove), because of the malignant monsters that dwelt therein. His family was comprised of three persons, his son Sunfells, his fair daughter Miniota, and his wife.

"He told his son Sunfells not to go upon the creek when out on hunting expeditions, but always to return by land, lest the monsters should attack him. For some time Sunfells obeyed the wishes of his father, but one day as he was returning home very late, being tired and hungry, he came to the margin of the stream, opposite his father's camp, and ventured to cross in his canoe. He had gone about half-way across the creek, when strange rumbling noises were heard from the bottom, the creek began to rise and become turbulent; and Sunfells became terribly afraid. He paddled for the opposite bank with all possible speed, but his canoe was over-turned and he was precipitated into the waters, where he soon perished. The chief was deeply enraged at the disobedience and loss of his son, and vowed eternal vengeance upon the manitous of the stream. Miniota was almost frantic with grief, and hardly could be restrained from throwing herself into the creek which was now lashed to a foam by the creatures within.

"The father determined to watch for a favourable opportunity in the morning to carry out this threat, when the monsters would leave the waters and seek repose upon the mossy banks.

"At the break of day, he took his bow and arrows and went to the creek to execute his project. Lest he should be detected he hid himself in a hollow pine tree, near the bank.

Not till noon did the monsters issue forth, and laid themselves down upon the soft, warm moss, where, not being used to the heat of the sun, they were soon overcome by a deep sleep. The chief now took careful aim with his bow and flint-pointed arrow, and seriously wounded one of the water deities. Aroused from their sleep, they were terribly enraged, and plunged into the water, which they agitated until it arose, overflowed the banks, carrying everything away in its course.

"Kiotsaton took refuge, in company with Miniota, on a high bank nearby, and waited for the subsidence of the waters, which had washed away his wife and camp. While deeply meditating upon his losses, he saw Glooskap, the "kind manitou," speeding towards him, who informed him that the spirits of the stream would have to be appeased in their wrath by the offering of his daughter, the fair Miniota. The father entreated the manitou to allow him to give himself as an offering, instead of his favourite daughter, but without avail. The manitou had spoken.

"Miniota, who through weariness had fallen asleep, was now awakened by the sobs of her father, and not knowing of the visit of Glooskap, inquired the nature of his great grief. Kiotsaton unfolded to her the decision of the manitou, and, after performing some Indian rites, she urged her father to allow her to offer her life as a sacrifice to the angry monsters; and as the grief-striken chief covered his emotions and tears from her, she silently slipped from the banks to the troubled waters below. The monsters at once carried her to the bed of the creek, near where her father's wigwam once stood; where she became the unwilling bride of the chief manitou, Ossossane.

"The rage of the monsters of the stream being now appeased, the waters sought their original level, and flowed as smoothly as before the onslaught on their sacred persons. Kiotsaton, who could not bear to be away from the place, the scene of his awful calamity, rebuilt his wigwam near the site of his old one, and became a noted sorcerer of his race; Glooskap again appearing to him and telling him that the spirit of his loved Miniota would come back to this world again, and reside in a great stone near the stream, where her spirit would minister to the afflicted of her race, continuing her deeds of mercy, till the stream became dried up.

"For some years afterwards Kiotsaton lived with the brethren on the banks of the Minnewauken, and many were the cures that he effected, by the aid of his famous medicine-stone, containing the spirit of Miniota. He was at last stricken and died, leaving the spirit of Miniota encased in stone as a lasting tribute to her memory, and for the healing of his brethren. The stone was sacredly kept and guarded by the Indians, being in the custody of the medicine-men of the tribe, and handed down, the one to the other, and placed by them at stated seasons by the side of the stream for the healing of the people.

"Such was the legend of the fair Miniota as told to Ralph Thompson by the aged Indian. The story was fascinating, and though in many ways crude, it reveals a wealth of imagination, and strength of intellect that points to a period of culture and years of enlightenment in the history of the noble red man "who sees God in clouds, or hears Him in the winds.""

There are differences in the details of the healing-stone in the following legend. The spelling is slightly different and the stone lies within the waters of a pool, yet the similarities tie the two tales together. Perhaps in the years between the two, circumstance changed these details.

La Belle Marie
Burned at the Stake

There are many many wonderful legends which come to us from the Micmac of days past. This one was found in an old Micmac prayer book, which was placed in the Smithsonian Institute by Frank Deedmeyer, formerly American Consul in Charlottetown. It was apparently given to the American Consul by an elderly Indian, Sosep, who said priests wrote the prayers in Micmac characters and the story of La Belle Marie was composed by a missionary of the Brotherhood of Port La Joie. The story, which appears on the inside front cover, is written in French.

Before reading the story of La Belle Marie, readers would be well advised to read the Micmac legend of the Stone of Mineota which precedes this story.

La Belle Marie's story begins with her parents, one Captain Granville and his wife, a woman who worked alongside her husband in what was termed dangerous enterprises and helped him bury most of their treasure along the shores of the Gulf of Mexico. Just where the ship captain and his Mrs. obtained these treasures no one is certain, but the implication was that he was a pirate.

Madame Granville found herself alone when the Captain set sail for South America and never returned. The widow, a

woman of masculine appearance and, it seems, determination for adventure decided to seek out her Basque relatives.

Her quest brought her to the Island. The year was 1721
and Marie was 15 years old. The two women were quickly
accepted by the French and Indians, who delighted in
Marie's dancing and song. Marie, it appears must have been
a talented young woman for she spoke Spanish, English,
French and it seems she was quickly conversing in Micmac.
She loved the Indian ways and learned to shoot the bow and
joined in their dances.

One particular chief and his son, Kaktoogwasees, became enraptured by Marie.

The two women spent more and more time with the
Micmac. Madame Granville was particularly entranced by
a famous spring, near St. Peters, it was the one known to
the French as La Grande Source. To the Micmacs the spring
was home of supernatural events and, being much revered,
the topic of many strange tales. Because of those tales the
superstitious French became afraid of the women and began to avoid them. A fact which caused them to draw closer
and closer to the Micmac chief and his son.

So captivated did they become that the betrothal of Marie
and Kaktoogwasees was announced in the autumn, during
a farewell feast held to send the hunters off to the mainland.
All were not pleased, some felt the chief's son should marry
a woman of his own race. Regardless, plans went ahead.

The next spring Marie and Mrs. Granville travelled down
river to Port La Joie and from there it was planned that
Madame would journey to the Gulf of Mexico to retrieve a
dowry suitable for one marrying a man of high rank. Marie
was to meet her intended.

Evil forces were at work for the next day Kaktoogwasees
spotted their empty canoe from where he awaited Marie's
arrival. Madam Granville was found scalped on the bank of
the river. Her daughter, the fairy-like Marie lay beside her,
near death.

All of the nursing skills of Kaktoogwasees' mother could

not revive her, nor could the ways of the medicine man. After weeks the old Chief was desperate. He called for the stone of Mineota to heal his son's bride.

The tribal elders and medicine man were enraged. They believed the stone which lay at the bottom of La Grande Source, was only to be used for those of Micmac blood, and would loose its power if used on Marie.

Their objections could not shake the determination of the old chief so the next day Kaktoogwasees, his father and council went to the spring. The young chief plunged into the icy waters through the bubbling pool and surfaced holding the sacred Mineota in his hands. Quickly they took the stone to Marie and began rituals led by the medicine man. After drawing a circle around the stone and filling it with maize, dried berries, trinkets and ornaments they walked around it nine times, calling on Mineota, the spirit of the stone. Marie was moved near and her right hand placed on the stone.

She immediately showed signs of recovery, slipping into a natural healing sleep. Marie quickly recovered, but the stone was lost to the Micmac for when Kaktoogwasees went to lift it from the ground to return it to the pool it turned to dust in his hands.

The near loss of his bride-to-be stirred the young chief to advance the date of the wedding. All of the ancient rites and ceremonies of the Micmacs were to be performed at the nuptials. A bower decorated with nature's finest was assembled before the chief's wigwam and here, before the members of the tribe Marie and Kaktoogwasees exchanged vows.

But before they could even step from the bower an arrow ran straight and true from the forest to pierce the heart of the young chief. He died held to the breast of his beloved Marie. The act was probably one of retaliation against a chief who had broken the rules of his tribe.

Marie was shunned and eventually left the tribe to wander amongst sailors and fishermen. Tales of her supernatural powers and practice of sorcery spread until finally complaints were heard by the Intendant at Port La Joie. It is said that he, being assured that the welfare of the new settlement and faith of the Micmac were endangered by a woman now termed a wicked sorceress, brought Marie to trial for Witchcraft early one November.

She was sentenced to suffer death at the stake on the morning of the 17th of that month.

Yet even death in the flames was not enough to silence La Belle Marie. It is said that a young soldier posted as a guard on the eve of her execution was never allowed to rest in peace. That night Marie sang her wild, plaintive songs until she had his attention, then begged the young man to set her free and flee with her to seek her father's buried treasure.

The young French soldier was tempted but heeded warnings about her bewitching spells making men do evil deeds and left her imprisoned.

The next day she was tied to a stake driven into the ground between Point de la Flame and the Black Cross, an area now known as Rocky Point. And, the young Frenchman watched her burn, singing her songs. He ran from the scene and wandered aimlessly until found days later. He claimed to hear the melody of Mineota all of his life, plagued with it even on his deathbed.

Did racial bigotry and misunderstanding of a fey teenager bring about such unhappiness? Or was Marie truly evil, bringing the wicked ways of her father to her own generation? We will never know. Perhaps if you go to the shore area of Rocky Point, where the winds blow over the cliffs, you will join those who claim to have heard the song of La Belle Marie.

Miminegash

These stories were told to a writer by the name of Helen Jean Champion who visited Prince Edward Island as a single woman in the mid-1930s. An adventurous sort, she bicycled around the province alone and left the story of her journey to be treasured by us all in a book called, Over On The Island *published in 1939.*

He Who Walks the Lights of the Northern Sky

This tale was related to her by a fisherman, sitting on the end of the Miminegash wharf.

"Many long years ago there lived an old, old Indian in this district of Miminegash. He was so very old that none of the other warriors could remember him as anything but old. Even the bears of the forest and the lobsters which crawled in the sea addressed him as 'Father.' To him the Manitou had given the secret of the winds, and the lightning, the rain and the trees. Night after night he would wander around when all others were asleep, and speak with the spirit of the stars. The birds came at his call, and even the timid wood mouse followed him serenely happy in his company. He was old, so very, very old …

"One day the Spirit of the Sea called to him ... What the Spirit told him no one knows. But, as the Indians gathered together on the shore that evening, they saw the Old Father step into his canoe. Silently he sat in the bow, looking intently out beyond the horizon ... Then, the boat began to move. Some unseen force seemed to draw the frail craft out, out into the Strait. Farther and farther it went. Then, suddenly a heavy mist descended on the sea like a vast curtain ... The boat passed through it and the old Indian was gone.

"The Indians mourned. They felt lost without their gentle old father. For weeks they grieved. For weeks they wandered along the shore looking always out, out over the Strait. Their hunting was neglected. Their wigwam fires died down unnoticed. Still they haunted the shoreline looking in vain for a frail canoe to come in over the sea.

"Finally, one night, as the stars twinkled faintly in the sky, a vast panorama of moving lights appeared. These shifting lights were not new, but this time there was something unusual about them. The Indians had seen them many times before, so that now they scarcely noticed them. Suddenly, a weeping brave exclaimed:

"Look! Look!"

"There, amid the shifting lights, stood the old Indian, with one arm stretched protectingly over them. Around him were grouped his friends of the forest and the field. And as they stood in awe and fear, the old Indian spoke to them.

"'My children,' he said, 'I have dwelt with you ever since your forefathers left the plains of Asia and wandered across this trackless land of the setting sun. Now, that is all over. Another race will sweep into this land and take possession of the country. But you will not be left alone. For every year I will walk amid the changing lights of the northern sky.' The lights flashed again, grew dimmer, and faded away ...

"The indians returned to their wigwams satisfied. The Indians understood."

Refugee's Revenge

Having finished his tale, the old tar on the wharf quickly began another.

"For many long years before the English came to the district of Miminegash, the Indians and French wandered unmolested and happily through this section of the Island. At that time the forest extended down to the sea, the shore was low, and the game plentiful.

"It was a lonely shore ... a peaceful life ... and all were happy until, one day, a French trader came with disturbing news. The British had taken Isle St. Jean. They were deporting the French inhabitants. The trader's wife and children had been taken. He himself had escaped with difficulty. The Indians must help to get back his family; if not, to get his revenge.

"Carefully they plotted. Many were the suggestions, but all were rejected except one put forward by a young and daring brave. For a few years they would wait until the new British settlers began to come in, then they would creep up on each new home and assassinate all the occupants. It was a satisfying scheme though it took so long.

"Year after year passed. Still, the trader and the braves waited for their revenge.

"Finally, the day dawned.

"Six canoes, with two in each, left the waters of Miminegash in search of revenge. Swiftly they paddled. The sky lowered threateningly. Still, they kept on, oblivious of their danger. Suddenly, with a loud crash, the storm broke loose and poured its wrath on the luckless voyageurs. The six canoes overturned. And only one man was left clinging to the canoe — the trader himself. What would have happened is evident. The trader was saved only by the intervention of a strong arm pulling him into a heaving rowboat. Then he knew no more, no more for ten long days.

"The man who he had planned to kill had saved him

instead. The thought burned itself into the trader's fevered brain. Not only did he save him but, during the long hours of his convalescence, he changed his spirit. Years later, when troops were recruited to fight against the invading Americans, the trader and the Scotsman marched to battle together. The trader's revenge was completed.

" 'I fight with the English against the English,' he said, and laughed mirthlessly."

The Phantom Ship of Northumberland Strait

As far back as 1786 there have been reportings of a
phantom ship appearing at various places in the 130-
mile long Northumberland Strait. Many of these
accountings are documented in various books and articles,
some, it is to be granted, with much scepticism. Others are
reported factually in a manner that suggests the writer gives
some credence to those telling the tale.

The first documented sighting, in 1786, occurred at Sea
Cow Head Lighthouse. The keeper watched in horror as a
three-masted schooner, sails full and swollen by the terrible
winds of a northeast gale, drove in closer and closer to the
treacherous rocks at the base of the cliffs.

Just as all seemed hopeless, the ship turned into the storm
and was lost to sight in the rain squall.

Reports have continued from that day to this. In fact the
most recent report came just as I was finishing this book in
January, 1988, when a burning ship was spotted just off
Borden from the ferry. Although the ship's radar was di-
rected at the vision, it was not detected on the instruments.

Captain Angus Brown of Wood Islands recalled that he
and his crew had taken the ferry Prince Nova out from
Wood Islands one night to bring aid to a ship that appeared
to be burning. As they approached, it vanished. A couple
near Glengarry saw the burning full-rigged ship from their

bedroom window. It was sailing northward at impossible speed. They did not raise an alarm as they knew what it was, but were able to watch it for more than an hour.

Many times boatsmen have set out to the ship, either with the intention of rescue, or to solve the mystery of the ship which has plied the strait for so many years. A fisheries' patrol vessel sighted it off the west end of the Island, but even with the speed of modern vessels, could not catch the elusive ship.

So real is the vision that at one time a group of men, including the late John P. MacLean, were working at their employment in the port of Charlottetown, when word was received of a ship in peril in Charlottetown Harbour.

"Some distance out in the channel was what appeared to be a large three-masted sailing vessel which was ablaze from bow to stern. Her crew were seen frantically running from one side of the ship to the other in their efforts to quell the many blazes which ravaged the vessel." (excerpted from Folklore of Prince Edward Island by Sterling Ramsay.)

A rescue boat began rowing to the scene in hopes of saving men from the water, but before they could arrive, mist engulfed the burning vessel and she was never seen again although a thorough search was made, even to sending divers to search the bottom. She was reported in the harbour on later occasions, still burning.

It was my intention to determine whether there have been any sightings of the phantom ship since 1900 and, if possible, talk with someone who had seen the ghost ship. The problem is not finding people who have seen the ship, but rather deciding whose accounting to include. Since the past is so well documented, I have focused on sightings by those alive today.

Carol Livingston and her sisters, of West Point, saw the phantom ship:

"It was really eerie. We thought at first it was New

Brunswick lights, but it was too close. Really couldn't have been a ship as the Strait was frozen solid — it was March in 1985."

Debbie Gamble-Arsenault, of Cross Roads, claims to have seen the phantom ship personally. The daughter of Aubrey and Jeanne Robinson of Alexandra, she grew up in the Alexandra/Tea Hill area. The sighting occurred in her sixteenth year (1970), when at church camp at Rice Point.

"St. Peter's Island was quite close to the camp. It was said you could walk across at low tide as the water was very shallow, but I never believed that. Anyway, one night several of us got up to go to the washrooms; they were in separate buildings. The other girls went outside before I did and I could hear them saying things like, "Oh wow!" and "What is it?"

When I went out, I saw they were looking at the burning ship, just off Robinson's Island. I couldn't tell if it was a three-masted ship or not, but the sails were up and people were running about on the deck, and it was burning. But it didn't get burned up."

When asked if frightened at such a sight, she said no. She had often heard the legend told in the community as she was growing up and just accepted it.

"Lots of people have seen it; I didn't think anything of it, and it didn't hang around long after I came out of the washroom, I only saw it about a minute. Enough to see it was a masted schooner, burning, and people on the deck."

A second source of information about the phantom ship was Elaine Monteith of Cornwall who comes from a seafaring family. Her maternal grandfather worked on the iceboats and her paternal grandfather was on a schooner.

She said her paternal grandfather (now deceased), often reported seeing the phantom ship in the Strait, and described the sighting in a similar way to other reports. He said it was often spotted just before a storm, and most often in October. He saw it in several locations along the Strait.

A more recent sighting was made by Elaine's uncle in 1954. A car, loaded with seven young people, was coming down Hampton Hill, when the occupants first saw the ship. All but two had heard the legend so were not afraid. The remaining two were amazed.

They followed the burning boat as far as DeSable, hoping to get a better view, but it never came any closer to shore. Her uncle described it as a sailing vessel with people running about on deck and climbing in the rigging. It was burning brightly, but never changed its physical appearance.

Rhonda Smallman saw the ship from the beach, up west, in the 60s. "Everyone saw it, the beach was full of people." It was about five in the evening, she recalled, describing both the burning three-masted schooner and people "coming off the front of it."

The general information in all accounts corresponded, with the exception of minor detail; some don't recall the people on deck, others did not recall flames. Sightings have been reported most in the spring and fall, but also in the summer, and even when ice is on the Strait. What is significant is the fact that everyone accepted it without fear or even disbelief. The result, I would assume, of the tradition of the story-teller in a family. Things repeated often enough, without a sense of fear, are simply accepted as part of life, even today.

Sea Cannon of the Strait

The occurrence of sonic booms, or cannon fire, has been reported many, many times in conjunction with sightings of the phantom ship. Of course, legend has it that the sea guns are fired by ghosts of the sailors, and are responsible for the circumstance of the phantom ship. These mysterious booms occur most frequently in the spring, and thus have been blamed on ice breaking up.

Those theories are themselves shot down, however, when the sound occurs at other times of year — as it does.

Whatever the significance of the sea gun-fire, it has been recorded on instruments as far away as New York.

Explanation

There is no explanation for the phantom ship, just numerous theories as to how she came to be. The most common is that a pirate made a pact with the devil to protect and hide his treasure from discovery. In return, the captain and crew were to sail forever on the burning ship. It is said that the pact was made when the ship, which had been fired upon, was burning to the waterline and would soon sink, taking all hands and the treasure in her holds to the bottom. Their fate was, many felt, just revenge for the terrible deeds they had done in their days of piracy on the high seas. Among those deeds were the execution of several children of the church, priests and nuns, bound on a mission of mercy.

It seems likely that many stories of the past were embellished with more frightening details as they were passed from story-teller to story-teller. After all, this was a form of recreation, an entertainment, made more enjoyable if a shiver could be sent up the spines of attentive listeners. Yet in the case of the phantom or burning ship, sightings have continued for 200 years. Who can call all of those folk, who tell you to your face of seeing this phenomenon, that you think them liars — not I!

The
Great Seal Robbery

Privateers ransacking the town, taking political prisoners, and threatening women and children! Not the kind of tale one associates with the history of the Island, yet it is a well-documented event.

On November 17th, 1775, Charlottetown was indeed under attack. That morning citizens awoke to find two strange vessels sailing into the harbour, preparing to fire on the town.

Governor Walter Patterson was in England, leaving Attorney General Phillips Callbeck in charge of the government. He had no soldiers and could not defend the town but, thinking the ships carried pirates who could be bribed to leave, he hurried to the wharf.

The ships, the *Franklin* and the *Hancock,* had been sent out from the United States in October under orders from General George Washington to stop British vessels and capture ships carrying soldiers, ammunition, or supplies which could be used against them during the American Revolution. As the thirteen colonies did not have a navy, they encouraged privateers, owned by private citizens, to fight for the cause at sea with a share of the booty as their reward.

Rules had been laid down forbidding attacks on settlements on land, but Captains John Selman of the *Franklin* and Nicholson Broughton of the *Hancock* chose to ignore them.

That late fall morning, Selman and a boatload of men landed on the wharf at the foot of Queen Street, were Callbeck stood waiting.

The Attorney General later documented the events that followed, giving a rather lurid account of the doings of these marauders. Strangely enough, he wrote his report in the third person.

"Mr. Callbeck met Selman on his landing who, notwithstanding a very civil reception, instantly ordered him to board one of the vessels, without permitting him to return to his house, though requested to do so; and as he was going aboard, one of the party insolently, without any provocation, struck him."

The boat's crew had been threatening the crowd on shore with their guns, and when one of the spectators objected, he was pushed into the boat with Callbeck and also taken prisoner.

In the meantime, Broughton had taken a boatload of privateers to Fort Amherst on the point. Finding it undefended, he did not attempt to take the cannon, but spiked them so that the British could not use the guns; then he rowed over to join Selman.

The two American captains and their crews proceeded to pillage the town. They went to the government storehouse and carried out nearly all the contents, which they transported to the hold of the *Franklin* ; then they broke into two other storehouses, from which they removed all the goods. One contained the supplies that had been collected for 103 new settlers who had arrived late in the season.

These people nearly starved to death during the following winter because their supplies had been stolen. They had to live on lobsters and shellfish gathered from the shore, and on potatoes that they traded from some Acadians in exchange for clothing brought with them from Scotland.

Next the Americans ransacked the Callbeck house, taking or smashing all they could find within.

Callbeck's report continued "... also all the porter, rum, geneva and wine (except one cask which they stove the head into and drank the whole out). At the same time they plundered the whole of Mrs. Callbeck's little stores of vinegar, oil, candles, fruit, sweetmeats, bacon, hams, etc. Not yet satisfied with wanton depredation, they next went to Mr. Callbeck's office, from which they took some of his clothes, etc., the Provincial Silver Seal, Governor Patterson's commission, two trunks full of goods, his clerk's desk and wearing apparel; opened Mr. Callbeck's bureau and desks, read all his papers, which were of great importance in his private concerns."

The Great Seal of the Colony, mentioned by Mr. Callbeck, had been issued to St. John's Island by King George III who is said to have suggested the design. On it were three small oak trees under a large oak tree to represent the three counties of the Island under the care of Great Britain. The seal had to be used on all laws and commissions of the time to make them legal.

"That after they had accomplished thus far of their cruelty, they made Mr. Wright a prisoner, and, with insulting language, laughed at the tears of his wife and sister, who were in the greatest agony of distress at so cruel a separation from their husband and brother." (Callbeck).

Mr. Wright had been one of Captain Samuel Holland's assistants during the survey, was a member of the governing council, and helped raise volunteers to go to Quebec to fight for the British.

By now it was late afternoon, so the captains returned to their schooners, leaving a party ashore to continue the destruction.

Another lady who was severely distressed at the privateers' actions was Mrs. Callbeck who was forced to flee through the woods to save her life.

"These monsters, blood-thirsty, sought out Mrs. Callbeck

for the purpose (to use their own words) of cutting her throat, because her father, a Mr. (Nathaniel) Coffin of Boston, is remarkable for his attachment to the Government (of Britain)." (Callbeck).

The next morning the two captains set sail before they could be caught by British warships, taking Mr. Wright and Mr. Callbeck as prisoners. They were at sea about two weeks, during which time they captured some fishing vessels and an English ship from London, all bound for the Island. Prisoners were taken, but all except a Mr. Higgins, the Island's newly appointed naval officer, were set free, and later reached Charlottetown in a small schooner — relieved of their possessions.

Upon reaching Maine, an officer, armed men, and fourteen prisoners, including Callbeck, Wright, and Higgins, marched about 120 miles down the coast to Cambridge (near Boston) — then the headquarters of the American Army. They were politely received by General George Washington who was angry at the way the two captains had carried out the mission.

"Indignant at the conduct of the two captains. 'The plague, trouble and vexation,' he wrote, 'I have had with the crews of all the armed vessels, are inexpressible. I do believe there is not on early a more disorderly set'." (Callbeck).

Washington freed the prisoners, ordering their property be given back to them; however, most of it had already been sold. He gave Mr. Callbeck permission to hire a vessel to take the Islanders home, but winter weather prevented them from getting back to the Island until the spring of 1776.

Aside from the loss of personal fortunes, those at home had suffered immeasurably from lack of supplies.

The Great Silver Seal was not returned to Callbeck, in spite of Washington's order, and has never been found. In all probability, it was melted down and made into silver coin. Fortunately, a wax copy of the seal had been made.

This was not the only association that Prince Edward Island had with privateers or pirates, but it seems to be the best chronicled.

Edward Hocking, author of Prince Edward Island, *a history book, tells readers that as a result of the incident the British despatched a sloop-of-war from Halifax to the Island, as well as four companies of soldiers to act as a garrison; however, before they could reach Charlottetown, the Malpeque area was raided by two more privateers, and so was St. Peters, where oxen and sheep were killed.*

A Pirate, Island Born

Several decades were to pass before an infant was born on the Island who would bring shame to his family for his dastardly deeds on the high seas.

S amuel Nelson was born during the era that saw the Great Seal pirated, the early 1800s. He came from a well-to-do family headed by one John Nelson, a land owner of note, who resided just outside of Charlottetown. Samuel had what would seem an ideal start in life. Upon his marriage, he was given a farm; he also was granted a military commission — situations that should have set him up for a genteel life many would envy.

But Samuel was of a different sort. Not for him the dull world of militia and farming. He longed for the excitement of the sea, the challenge of trade. And he decided to pursue those interests. For a time he was satisfied with a flourishing business, shipping goods between the Island and Halifax.

His commission served him well, opening doors that kept his brig steadily in service.

His longings for adventure, unfortunately, led Samuel to bedrooms other than his own, bringing disgrace on his head and causing the loss of the commission. Unrepentant, Samuel upped and left for more favourable circumstances, deserting his wife and brood of children in the process.

In Halifax he was granted another commission, but a

meeting with a privateer named Morrison cancelled out any thought of a respectable career. Combining Morrison's expertise with Samuel's money, the duo formed a partnership, purchased a sleek American sloop with at least ten mounted guns, and hired a crew eager for easier money then could be gained from the fishery.

The pirates captured a brig out of Europe, sold the ship and her cargo in New York, and were off on a career that took them to the West Indies and back up the eastern seaboard. They plundered both on-shore and off, making a great profit from their endeavours. Of course, the authorities were not sitting idly by. The pressure put on by pursuing government ships drove them into ever new waters.

Eventually their careers led them back to Samuel Nelson's home territory. They raided off the coast of Newfoundland, and even returned to Prince Edward Island where Samuel and his wife were reunited. It was here they met their comeuppance, at least to a degree. Morrison and several of the crew drowned when their vessel ran aground during dirty weather.

Lady Luck continued to smile on Samuel; he survived the wreck, gathered up his wife and children, and retired to a respectable career as a trader in New York, where his fortune provided a very pleasant life.

Second Sight Sally
Sees Doom For Snowdrift

There are literally hundreds of tales of shipwrecks and mysterious events concerning sailors. This one is included because of second-sighted Sally who forecast the fate of the Snowdrift.

On a clear day a small crowd gathered near Vernon off Orwell Bay for the departure of the ship, *Snowdrift,* on her maiden voyage. She was captained by one Rach Nelson, a young man of twenty-six, in command for only the second time in his career.

Snowdrift was said to be a beautiful vessel, "as graceful as a swan" as she moved away from the pier and sailed down the river. As she disappeared from view, second-sighted Sally gave her first ominous warning. She had, she said, heard a strong note in the cry of the sea-mews, raising concern about the fate of the ship and crew.

Time passed with no word from the ship, but Sally told of a dream she had of pirates attacking the *Snowdrift* and forcing the captain to walk the plank.

It was years before the tale was confirmed. A dying seaman, concerned about his admission through the pearly gates, confessed to being involved in the plundering of the *Snowdrift* and the murder of the crew — all for the gold she carried.

Winter — Kills Snow Squall

Another ship named for snow met an equally sad end. The *Snow Squall* seemed fated from its conception. Its keel was laid in a snowstorm; it was launched in a snowstorm; and it was lost in a snowstorm. The ship was built by the Crapaud Harbour.

Yet another from the same harbour was lost in 1815. A fine vessel called the *Seven Brothers,* she was moored waiting for rigging and cargo to be installed, when a severe autumn frost set in. She became firmly stuck in ice which, in December, carried the vessel out into the Strait. A volunteer crew went out to take the ship to Charlottetown; however, a violent storm with excessively high winds caused the hold to fill with water, forcing the crew out of their shelter and onto the deck, where they were exposed to the full force of the storm. Several died from exposure.

Buried Treasure

There are many tales of treasure being buried, and a few of it being found, around our Island shores. Most of the caches were close to the shores, for the simple reason that currency in the days when treasure was buried, was heavy. There was no paper money; all such assets were coin, gold, or other valuables. To maintain any secrecy at all, it must be buried within lugging distance of where a boat could be anchored.

Tales of pirates in the waters of the Gulf of St. Lawrence abound, so it is natural that thoughts turn to their treasure.

One who is often referred to in such tales is Captain Kidd, although he was hanged for piracy in 1700, about thirty-five years before the first white settlers arrived in many of the districts where treasure was thought to be. Perhaps the Micmacs are responsible for passing along tales of Kidd's exploits.

Whatever the origin of such stories, they certainly do abound. I have decided, in researching the matter, it is most likely that a number of pirates did indeed set foot on the Island. Most, because of the nature of their business, would have failed to introduce themselves, and because of the notoriety and — let's face it — romance associated with Captain Kidd, became collectively lumped under his name.

Or could the hangman have mistaken his victim, hanging, not the famous Kidd, but an unfortunate look-alike?

Not long after reports from England told of the hanging of Kidd for committing acts of piracy on the high seas, rumours began to circulate among the populace of St. John's Isle that a vast treasure was buried near Marshfield.

Story had it that the pirate had needed to stash numerous chests of gold coin, jewels, and other valuables, which made up the acquired loot from raids in the Caribbean. So successful had been the forays into battle that the sight of the skull and crossbones sent a shiver of doom down the spines of any who sighted it.

Kidd became a rich man, so rich many thought that even the King of England was involved in the piracy. When such rumours began to circulate in Britain, Kidd was brought to trial and quickly hanged. It is easy to believe that if a conspiracy with the King had existed, the pirate's life was spared, allowing a possible grain of truth to the stories of buried treasure that are documented throughout Atlantic Canada.

Kidd Holds To Agreement
No Human Sacrifice, No Treasure

An Island writer by the name of Allan MacRae documented this account of Kidd's ghost defending his treasure, just years after his reported hanging. The account was given to me by another collector of treasure stories from "Up West," who said that MacRae had used F. H. MacArthur's book, Pirate's Gold, *as his source of information.*

"A one-time resident of Marshfield, by the name of Hasket, Jim Hasket , dreamed just where the treasure lay, and so he and his neighbour, Bill Heeney, went in search of it. Hasket further claimed that he talked with Kidd in his dream and that the pirate told him the treasure was hidden near the shore near Marshfield. However, it was not to be lifted without a human sacrifice.

The two agreed to meet the following night, when the buccaneer would furnish further details, but before separating Kidd drew a wrinkled, yellowed paper from his bosom and handed it to the highly excited Islander. When the notorious captain disappeared, Hasket opened the faded paper with trembling hands and read the following words:

'No words must be spoken aloud during the time the treasure is being lifted and no lights of any kind are to be employed. At the stroke of midnight you'll see my ship offshore. You'll be able to recognize her by a large red light at the bow and the Jolly Roger at the mast. I will come ashore with a few men and together we'll complete the task.'

'It always had been an unwritten law among pirates that a human sacrifice be made when a hoard was buried and again when it was taken away. Obey this order, Hasket or suffer the consequences.' The letter was signed Captain Kidd.

The whole plan was carried out in strict secrecy. Not a soul in Marshfield save Hasket, Heeney and two other men, knew anything about the strange affair, and these were sworn on blood oath to keep mum.

One fellow aboard Kidd's ship had been instructed to give three shrill blasts on a horn when the midnight hour arrived. A great silence came over the treasure seekers as the zero hour approached for Captain Kidd to show up drew near. Everyone stood tense. Hasket was the most excited of them all, and when midnight had passed without Kidd showing up he became very angry and cried out in a loud voice.

'Bill Kidd I command you in the name of Beelzebub to appear and deliver the goods'.

There was no reply. The failure of the pirate ship to appear was a great disappointment to the waiting men; yet there was hope, and following the example of their leader, they began digging furiously in the spot where Hasket thought the fortune might lay.

When the diggers had gone down some ten feet or so, water from the nearby river began to flood the hole. It was well after the witching hour when a bloodcurdling yell rent the air and put the fear of the Lord into the diggers.

What could it be? Where did the sound come from? None of the group waited to find out. In the wildest disorder, spades were tossed aside and the gold seekers fled for their lives.

Never again could any of them be persuaded to visit the place, no not for all the riches of Captain Kidd!"

DeRoma's Gold

Many renditions of buried treasure stories were passed down through families or by story tellers. Mrs. L. E. Mac-Gowan wrote an account of a story told her by her father, Col. Weatherbie, whose mother was one of the youngest of the Parker family referred to below. Mr. Parker and a neighbour, Dr. Kaye, were said to have seen where treasure digging had taken place at the small island off Point DeRoma.

The first Parker, George, immigrated from Ireland via Newfoundland where he found his bride. The couple arrived in Georgetown in 1827 and made their home at Franklin Hill farm on a point of land at the east entrance to the Brudenell River.

The talk of pirates and treasure must have been ongoing in the area for many holes were dug along the shore line property on Franklin Hill Farm. That activity, combined with the romantic stories that would have been told of the DeRoma fort and settlers, made it natural that some of Mr. Parker's fifteen children (it took him three wives to gain such a large family) should be interested in treasure.

The DeRoma settlement began in 1734 as part of the French plan to colonize Isle St. Jean. In spite of many setbacks, the settlement was thriving when, in 1754, DeRoma's fleet left the village for a fishing trip. While they were gone, American vessels anchored in the harbour and virtually wiped out the settlement by putting torch to everything that would burn, including buildings and crops in the field. France and America were at war at the time.

The event so thoroughly disheartened Count DeRoma and his citizenry that they departed.

Decades later French warships would visit Georgetown and various officers were welcomed into the Parker home. Talk, it is said, often turned to treasures and treasure hunting, and the boys told of the efforts of locals to find the bounty they were sure was buried in the area. They even bragged of a local spot where they were sure the catch was buried.

A huge boulder near the shore was certain to cover treasure, they thought. It was much too heavy for the lads to move, but they were convinced that when they could tip it over they would be rich; it was an idea they should have kept secret! The theory was that when DeRoma's settlers fled they could not carry heavy coin or gold, so it must have been hidden. The boulder was a logical place, for it was a good marker, easily spotted, yet too large and heavy to be moved. The refugees eventually got to Quebec, and DeRoma never again visited island shores — at least not to anyone's knowledge. In the 1800s, however, the last French warships to visit Georgetown for a number of years slipped quietly into the harbour one evening. Diverting from usual practice, they anchored in the Brudenell River, near where the boulder lay. The next morning they sailed without communicating with anyone in the community, greatly puzzling the inhabitants.

The Parker boys, however, solved the riddle of the mysterious visit, for when next they visited the boulder, it was to find that it had been overturned. An impression underneath in the shape of a large iron pot convinced them that their treasure had been "pirated by a French man-o'-war — and this in a time of peace," in the words of L. E. MacGowan.

Of course, it is speculation to assume that it was DeRoma gold, for if it was, it had been hidden for a century. Yet it could have been that the descendants of those who fled just needed the unintentional help of the Parker boys to locate a treasure of which they had heard recounted in tales handed down through generations.

Blue's Cove Treasure

No one seems sure just where the hint of treasure at Blue's Cove originated. The cove, located on the upper reaches of the Elliott which empties into Hillsboro Bay, was said to be a natural place to hide goods — easily identified, approachable, and yet rarely visited by local folk.

The notion of treasure led a local doctor, who had great affiliations with the sea and seafarers, to organize a group to excavate near the shore of the cove, close to the landing stage.

Story-teller Walter Shaw tells us that digging operations were conducted according to the superstitious notions of the day: "...in utter silence, in the dead hours of the night, and by the fitful light of a half-moon." Presumably these strict observances were to avoid waking the spirits connected with the treasure.

Apparently, without any known reason, shovels and picks were suddenly downed and the seekers fled the region never to be heard of again. Speculation has it that as they discovered proof that they were indeed onto a find, they broke their silence in the excitement of the moment. Is it possible that an apparition, resembling a buccaneer of days past, could have frightened them away? Sword dripping blood, did his laughter ripple to their very hearts, driving the diggers away over hill and dale, never to return? All that is known is that they did indeed disappear.

Walter Shaw speculates that local lads frightened the diggers away by hurling rocks, one at a time, into the midst of their labours. And yet, one must wonder why the rock throwers remained silent. Stranger yet is the fact that several folk, including the good doctor, were so frightened they disappeared. Would a few thrown rocks have managed that?

West Point

There are many versions of treasure seekers losing their bounty by breaking the silence needed to avoid the spirits left to guard the loot.

In modern day Prince Edward Island one place has retained its ties to the days of pirates, treasure, and seafaring tales more than any other. West Point, in particular the area around the West Point Lighthouse, still attracts treasure seekers to this day. For those with a spirit of adventure, it's a great place to spend a few days. You can even sleep in the lighthouse, using your own imagination about the tales that are told in the area.

Shipwrecks, mysterious sightings, buried treasure are all part of the lore to be found at the lighthouse, which is today an inn, restaurant, and museum. One of the powers behind the preservation of the lighthouse, and the creation of the museum is a wonderful story-teller who agreed to share her version of the buried treasure of West Point.

Dig in the Dark of the Moon
by Carol Livingston

T he wind howled dismally through the tall trees behind the house, an open barn door shut swiftly now and then with a sudden crack like a pistol shot. Upstairs, inside the small dilapidated farmhouse, a man thrashed restlessly from side to side on his narrow, lumpy mattress.

Finally, tired of this, his stout, gray-haired wife, Mary, reached over and gave him a quick shake. "What is it, John? Fer mercy sake, yuh've kep' me awake this past two hours wi' all yer thrashin' about. Wake up and go ta sleep right!"

With a start and a wild look in his eyes, John sat bolt upright, striking his head on the sloping roof in the process. "My God, Mary, I've jest hed a nightmare — yuh can't imagine what I saw jest now!"

"Well, since yuh kep' me awake fer the past two hours wi' yet thrashin' an' yer moanin' I guess yu'd better tell me about it."

Still shaking, John crept out of bed and lit the oil lamp. Together, glancing fearfully over their shoulders, they made their way down the creaky stairs to the kitchen. There by the flickering lamplight, he began to tell her of his dream, the words tumbling over one another in their eagerness to come out.

"I saw a black ship, Mary, a pirate vessel, come down in the Strait from the north — must uv been comin' from the Gulf er the Atlantic even! By the canvas she hed spread I'd say the cap'n figgured they wuz others not too far ahind. They wuz men along the side, Mary, keepin' watch fer a safe harbour. Fer a long spell, all they passed was high red capes; but after awhile the capes guv way ta sandy beaches. One uv the lookouts shouted — I could hear him plain as day, Mary — 'There's a cove ahead, Cap'n Kidd, jest beyon' the point' and, Mary, a man from below with a voice like a drum roared, 'We're goin' in, me hearties, fer if the King's men catch us with this load, we'll hang from the yard arm fer shur!' "

"Mary, yuh never saw such a band a cut-throats — big men they wuz an' ugly, but they wuz quick! Before yuh could hitch up a team a horses, they hed that big ship anchored in the cove an' then..." John babbled, his eyes big as saucers, "an' then they lowered a small boat with a man an' a boy in 'er. They wuz a big chest there, Mary, it must a bin a treasure chest."

"They rowed to the shore mighty fast. Whenever the boat touched the sand, the big man leaped into the tide-wash. He heaved the big chest to his brawny shoulders and strode toward the sand dunes, leaving tother 'un, a scrawny boy he wuz, about fourteen, to beach the boat and take the shovels. Jest beyond the sandhills they wuz three big pine trees, Mary, just like those big 'uns at your Paw's place. Well, the Cap'n plunked the chest down there an' tole the boy ta dig hard en fast if he knew whut wuz good fer him. Yuh never saw a boy whut could work so hard, Mary — why, in no time at all he had a great big hole dug, an' they put the chest in an' cuvered it up some fast. The cap'n tuk a big, mean lookin' knife from his belt an' blazed the three big pine beside the treasure. Then, quick as a cat, he grabbed the tired lad an' tied him to one 'a the trees."

" 'Yuh watch the treasure, lad, and them as tries to take it afore I come back 'ill die fer their greed!'

"He left him there, Mary, tied to a tree, beggin' an' screamin' and being almost eaten by the mosquitoes that swarmed around him. He'll die, Mary! He'll die!"

"Fer mercy sake, John, get a grip on yer senses! Twasn't nothin' more 'n a bad dream, tho' yuh almost had me believin' it fer a minute, whut with this wild storm an' all. Get back ta yer bed, man, there's wood to be chopped fer Rob in the mornin'!"

They climbed the narrow steep steps and lay down on their lumpy mattress, but there was precious little sleep for either of them that night. Visions of what they could do with the riches in the chest danced before their eyes — a decent house, their very own farm, and maybe even enough left over for a decent mattress.

Bright and early, John ate his porridge and molasses, and hurried up the road to Rob's to help in the wood cutting frolic. That day he did more talking than cutting, but no one seemed to mind. The idea in everyone's mind was finally expressed by one old chap who said, "Yuh know, they's bin a heap a people here on P.E.I. whut found money whut was buried by pirates. Seems to me there jest might be somthin' in that dream a yours."

The idea was much discussed all day and again at supper-time, when the men sat at the table eating fried pork and baked beans, washed down with lots of scalding hot tea. After supper, John went home through the gathering dusk, glancing fearfully over his shoulder now and then, as though expecting to feel the Captain's iron grip on his shoulder at any moment.

Shortly after getting home, John and Mary went to bed, tired out from their disturbed slumbers of the night before. About midnight, John sat bolt upright, striking his head again, and grabbed Mary by the shoulder. "They did it again, Mary, they did it again! I could hear the boy, Mary, a beggin an' a pleadin' fer the Cap'n to come back."

A third night John had the strange dream again and, by this time, he and some of his neighbours were convinced that it was more than just a dream. They hired a boat and began to sail around the Island, looking for a cove shaped like a half moon. For days they sailed along the coast, hailing every ship they met, to inquire about such a cove. At last, one day they sailed around North Cape and down the Northumberland Strait past high red cliffs, till they came to the gently sloping sand dunes of West Point. As they sailed carefully over the reef, John looked at the cove spread before them, shaped exactly like the one he had seen in his dream. "We've found the spot, men! We've found 'er!"

With hands a-tremble from eagerness, mixed with dread, they lowered the small boat and rowed awkwardly ashore. Once there, they scrambled over the sandhills, and began to look for the three blazed pines. They weren't long finding them, and sure enough, the three large marks put there by Captain Kidd's knife proclaimed this as the treasure site!

The men were eager to begin digging, but John held them back — "The dream tuk us this far, lads, and it's best we do whut the boy told me in me last dream. He said to dig at night, boys, in the dark of the moon. Remember now, yuh can't say nary a word 'er it will disappear on yuh. He said they wuz a curse on 'er; but I tell yuh, boys, I'm willin' ta risk it. The way we poor folks live is jest a curse anyways!"

They settled back to wait for darkness to fall, their talk a mixture of hope for the riches so near at hand, and terror, lest the curse come true.

The mist rolled in from the sea as darkness fell, and from the nearby marsh a loon gave its strange wild cry. In dead silence, the men picked up their shovels, walked silently to the trees and began to dig. For a time, the only sounds to be heard were the waves washing the shore, the grinding of the shovels digging in the damp sand, and the laboured breathing of the men, then came the indescribable and long-awaited sound of a shovel hitting the solid oak chest.

"We've got 'er, boys! We've got 'er!" rang the loud cry from someone's throat. At that very instant, the sand began to slide into the hole around the men so quickly they were almost trapped. From the cove came the sound of anchor chains being hoisted. The terrified men rushed to the cove in time to see through the lifting mist a sleek black pirate ship put out to sea. A hoarse voice floated back across the waves: "You've guarded it well, boy. You've guarded it well!" and with that the vessel vanished into the darkness.

In the nights that followed, many people tried their luck, but the result was always the same. Someone would forget and speak, and the treasure would disappear.

When the lighthouse was built in 1875, my great-grandfather became the keeper for fifty years. My grandfather says he can remember many times when people stayed at the lighthouse (West Point), while they waited for darkness to fall, so digging could begin. So many holes were dug that it became difficult to tell just where one should dig, so one enterprising man obtained a metal diviner, similar to a water wand, and sure enough, it quivered and shook and pointed to the ground at the very spot the old-timers maintained was the correct location.

At least one death was caused by the treasure hunt. One

of the diggers caught pneumonia and died almost immediately after digging. Another man fell from a roof and
was killed just after he, too, had been digging.

These two deaths caused a certain amount of belief in
"The Curse," and the lack of success finally caused many
to doubt the existence of the treasure. Those who dug were
ridiculed, and so the digging stopped until about ten years
ago. The modern treasure hunters were no more successful
than those of long ago; so there the treasure still lies there,
buried deep in the sand, just back from the half moon
cove, across the beach and over the dunes. Do you dare to
dig in the dark of the moon?

Cape Le Force

*Entered according to Act of Parliament, in the year 1893,
by Elizabeth S. MacLeod. In the Office of the Minister of
Agriculture. The book* Carols Of Canada *etc. etc. was re-
leased in Charlottetown, P.E.I. This poem is one of Mrs.
MacLeod's and details a crime, "...the first to blight
Prince Edward Isle," at Cape Le Force.*

> Where frowning bulwarks guard the coast
>   Around our sea-girt Isle.
> Where wildest winters wreak their wrath,
>   And sweetest summers smile.
>
> In holy calm of eventide
>   Which crowned the sunbright day,
> We sat upon a grassy knoll
>   That overlooked the bay.
>
> All glorious the lingering light
>   From out the radiant west,
> As loath to leave a scene so fair,
>   Illumined ocean's crest.

Along the path, with quiet tread,
　　There came an aged form
Whose sunburnt features told that he
　　Had weathered many a storm.

He'd held command in goodly craft
　　On nigh and far off seas;
Had furled the sail on foreign strand,
　　And scoured 'fore every breeze.

Now, 'yond all lure of worldly wealth
　　Through commerce on the foam,
He anchored where affection set,
　　Within his childhood's home.

Nor tide, nor wind, nor black storm-cloud
　　Could bar his passage more,
As he waited sailing orders
　　For glad Beulah's shore.

We asked him, as he rested near,
　　If he the story knew
Of that bleak, lonely cape which stretched
　　Upon our right hand view.

"I can relate," he said, "the tale
　　My grandsire told to me:-
It happened in the year of grace
　　Seventeen sixty-three.

"That year the Isle of St. Jean
　　Was ceded, this you know,
To Britain, in the treaty signed
　　By France, at Fontainebleau.

"French privateers, which robbed our coast,
　　Were harassed by our men;
McKenzie, with a British sloop
　　Unaided, captured ten.

"One, fleeter than the rest escaped,
    Commanded by Le Force;
In dread of foes, or unknown seas,
    He held a leeward course.

"But all too fast the gallant ship
    Bore down towards the bay;
Caught on deceitful shifting sands,
    A stranded wreck she lay.

"The boats made shore, the crew dispersed,
    One officer remained
With his commander, and large share
    Of ill-won booty gained.

"On yonder cape they pitched a tent,
    And from the vessel's store
In haste, with slightest interval,
    Much precious freight they bore.

"But where 'twas hid no mortal knew;
    Folk say within yon grove,
Whose crowding giants dull the day,
    Exists the treasure-trove.

"Be't so or not, to me it seems
    This cursed greed of gold
Shuts all the finer feelings out,
    Deforms life's fairest mould.

"Rends rare affection's dearest ties,
    Transforms the friend to foe;
In battlefield of worldly gain
    Smites with unsparing blow.

"Repels all humanizing love;
    In haste to reach its goal,
Draws even from gates of paradise
    The earnest, God-ward soul.

"Two daring youths, from hamlet nigh,
　　Through motives curious, went
When friendly even lent its shades,
　　Anear the strangers' tent.

"They heard dispute o'er money hoard,
　　Then louder, wrathful tones,
Which hotter, higher, waxed until
　　They sunk in low, faint moans.

"Next morn three sturdy fishermen
　　Steered out across the wave;
They heeded not the swelling surge,
　　Their hearts were firm and brave.

"But, Oh! what vision met their gaze!
　　Upon that silent shore
The Captain of the stranded bark
　　Lay stiffening in his gore.

"Far from his loved in La Belle France,
Far from his native plain;
Where longing eyes, and yearning hearts
Might long for him in vain.

"He died not as the soldier dies;
　　For country and for king;
For him no martial banners wave,
　　No lyre his praise doth sing.

"Rough hands, but souls of sympathy,
　　Entombed him where he fell;
While sounding ocean wailed his dirge,
　　And wavelets rang his knell.

"Now, until ocean yields her dead,
　　Till dries yon river's source,
That cape, baptized with his blood,
　　Shall bear the name 'Le Force.'"

He paused. "What of the murderer?
  And what to him befell?
He fled, from that dread hour of guilt
  No tongue his fate could tell.

"No legal technicality
  Could paint his black as white,
Or colour with a golden tinge
  The blackness of his night.

"Though richly-garbed, accomplished vice
  May bide the Final Day;
With brutal, prompt, unstudied crime
  The law brooks no delay.

"His was no deed of villain art
  Which slowly works its will,
Which wiles its victim to his death,
  And slays with callous skill.

"It may be that a Higher Judge
  Could measure best his crime;
And that, through penitence he found
  Pardon and peace in time."

The sun had sunk beneath the wave,
  The moon had risen on high;
And glorified, with silvery beams,
  The earth, and sea, and sky.

Light zephyrs thrilled on ocean's chords,
  Through wavelet's hum and flow;
Alas! that scene surpassing fair,
  Should sin or sorrow know.

Alas! that guilt, or causeless woe
  Should darken nature's smile;
As that foul deed, the first to blight
  With crime Prince Edward Isle.

The Murder of Abel

In 1901, Joe Brown, 103 years of age, was considered the authority on "The Capes." He had in his possession a copy of an old gazette published on the Island in 1816, which contained an advertisement for a reward of fifty pounds for the apprehension of one Pat Pierce, who was wanted for murder.

"This 'ere paper brings back to mind the story of the murder of Abel many long years ago," said old Joe Brown, relating that one Frank Midmay had written an accounting which began putting the pieces of the puzzle, that was the murder, into place. Using that account and his own knowledge, C. P. Flocton recounted the event in the PEI Island Magazine *of 1901. We have excerpted from that.*

"The frigate that I was to join came into the harbour soon after I reached Halifax. I went on board the frigate, where I presented my introductory letters to the nobleman who commanded her. I expected him to have been an effeminate young man, much too refined to learn his business; but I was mistaken. Lord Edward was a sailor every inch of him; he knew a ship from stem to stern, understood the character of seamen and gained their confidence. He was, besides, a good mechanic, a carpenter, ropemaker, sailmaker and cooper. He could hand, reef and steer, knot and splice; but he was no orator; he read little and spoke less. He was a man of no show, nor could you ever perceive any assumption of consequence from his title of nobility. We were not allowed to remain long in this paradise of sailors, being ordered suddenly to Quebec.

"We had not been long at sea before we spoke an Irish Guineaman from Belfast, loaded with emigrants for the United States; about seventeen families. These were contraband. Our captain had some twenty thousand acres on the Island of St. John's or Prince Edward's, as it is now called, a grant to some of his ancestors which had been bequeathed to him, and from which he had never received one shilling rent, for the very best reason in the world, because there were no tenants to cultivate the soil.

"It occurred to our noble captain that this was the very sort of cargo he wanted, and that these Irish people would make good clearers of his land. He made the proposal, and as they saw no chance of getting to the United States, and provided they could get nourishment for their families it was a matter of indifference to them where they colonized, the proposal was accepted, and the captain obtained permission of the admiral to accompany them to the Island, to see them housed and settled. Indeed nothing could have been more advantageous for all parties; they increased the scanty population of our own colony, instead of adding to the number of our enemies. We sailed again from Halifax a few hours after we had obtained the sanction of the Admiral, and, passing through the beautiful passage between Nova Scotia and the Island of Cape Breton known by the name of the Gut of Canso, we soon reached Prince Edward's Island.

"We anchored in a small harbour near the estate, on which we found a man residing with his wife and family; this fellow (Abel) called himself the steward, and from all I could see of him during our three weeks stay he appeared to be rascal enough for the stewardship of any nobleman's estate in England."

During their stay, the crew cut down trees and built log-houses for the new tenants. They "cleared, by burning and rooting up, as much land as would serve to sustain the colony for the ensuing season; and, having planted a crop of corn and potatoes, and given the settlers many articles useful in their new abode, we left them agreeable to our orders." At this point the accounting was taken over by Mr. Flocton who received more of his information from J. C. Underhay of Bay Fortune.

"It may fairly be surmised that much of the trouble between landlord and tenant that so long agitated the people of Prince Edward's Island and which makes up so large a portion of the history of the Province was due to the harshness of land agents in enforcing the payment of rents, much of which is supposed, in many cases, never to have reached the owners of the land, who were led to believe that the land was of little value.

"Edward Abel enjoyed as one of these land-agents a most unsavoury reputation, but many of his high-handed and outrageous acts can be traced directly to his wife's influence. She was a veritable virago, and urged her husband to commit many acts of oppression.

Art thou afear'd
To be the same in thine own act and valour
As thou art in desire?
"He was weak enough to submit,
Letting I dare not waitin upon I would
Like the poor cat i' the adage,
and she finally drove him to his doom. Pat Pierce, an honest, good fellow, owned what was very rare in those days, a thoroughbred horse. Mrs. Abel was violently jealous of this ownership, and set her wicked wits to compass its possession. Ready money was a rare thing among the farmers, so when Abel came down on Pierce unexpectedly for the payment of his rent, a sum of five pounds, eleven shillings, two pence, for his few acres, Pierce was put to some straits

to raise the money — there were no pawnbrokers on the Island in those days. He first disposed of many articles of comfort and necessity, and then sought among his neighbours to raise the balance. They willingly came to his assistance, for he was a good neighbour, and so he presented himself with the money at Abel's house, much to the disappointment of Abel's wife; but her covetous soul was equal to the occasion, it seems, for the money was refused on the ground that some of the coins were worthless. There being no bank in that part of the country, poor Pat was obliged to start on another pilgrimage to exchange the money. On return to his house his eyes met something that chilled his heart and fired his Irish temper. Edward Abel had seized his precious horse, and led him out by the halter. Pierce presented the money and demanded the horse. The former was refused and Abel held on to the horse.

"Pierce protested earnestly, but Abel was obdurate, and determined that the horse was now his, forfeit for unpaid rent. This was the grossest injustice, and more than Pierce's Irish blood could endure, for he saw through Abel's outrageous act the hateful purpose of the wife. He dropped the battle of words and went into the house, whence he immediately returned with one of those French muskets with bayonet* attached with which every settler was furnished by the Government. He gave Abel one more chance to take the money and release the horse. This he refused to do, and his high-handed and cruel nature got the check it richly deserved, for Pierce in a burst of indignation rushed at him with the bayonet and stabbed him twice — the last thrust a mortal would through the groin.

"Edward Abel's work of oppression and thieving was at an end. He managed to get as far as the Red House, which now gives its name to a locality near by. From this place a neighbour carried him home to his wife. It is to be hoped that the result of her wicked instigation brought home to this woman a lesson of humanity.

"Pat Pierce made good his escape, and the glittering

temptation of the reward of fifty pounds found no neighbour willing to betray Pat and accept the blood money."

The author of this piece claimed to be the proud possessor of this very bayonet (authenticated). "It adorns the beam over my ingle."

The first thoroughbred horses to be brought to Canada came to Prince Edward Island through the work of one of the governors and a wealthy British gentleman. The horses were envied by those far and wide, even to the extent where they were on occasion taken to Halifax to pull the carriage of dignitaries on state occasions. Thus, the ownership of such a rare breed was not only a symbol of place in the community, but also the potential for a good income for Pat Pierce. The legend says that the popular young man and his horse did not flee far, but their presence could never be found by the authorities because he was so well protected by all around him. It is to be sure that Pat Pierce became a legendary figure, because he was one of those who struck back at the frustrations and even, on occasion, corruptness, of the system of land ownership in early Prince Edward Island.

Abel's Cape

Charles Kent did not expect to encounter personally any of the traditions of the Island, such as finding buried treasure, but he did. In 1901, he related the tale of a bitter disappointment he experienced, which belied the fact that he had come to this Island, and indeed to Abel's Cape, for "health and recreation, and not for adventure."

"I can't say that I was ignorant of the Island's history, but it did not come into my mind again until long after my arrival; when I was slyly questioned by the inhabitants if I had come for the treasure — a local joke they spring on all visitors. I soon disabused their minds of being a treasure-seeker by roaming in the water with rod and creel in a quest of fish, being well rewarded for my long journey by the daily feasts of royal sea-trout, the beautiful scenery and the welcome knowledge that my health and strength were returning in speedy and ponderous proportions.

"But I have not yet stated where I am. This is Prince Edward Island, made famous by the novelist as the receptacle and hiding place of Captain Kidd's stolen hoards. The particular Cape I located on is the home of an old and dear friend, known to his intimates as "Flockie." It is called Abel's Cape. It runs into the sea from the mainland and rears itself by degrees out of the water to a height of fifty or sixty feet, its red rock and sand crowned with densely-growing fir, juniper and birch, making a gorgeous picture against the vivid sky and many tinted clouds.

"Only during the spring tides, when they are either very high or very low, is it possible to walk around the Cape by the beach, for with these exceptions the waves beat its base, washing away its body and undermining its green crown, which day by day drops off into the angry depths, carrying with it cords of its richly-scented timber. Periodically it is visited by wiseacres with divining rods, who have been prompted by dreams and prognostications to dig for Kidd's gold, many holes proving how firm is the belief that the treasure is buried here. The diggers, though, have not found it — they are always unsuccessful, and are usually scared away by the ghosts of Kidd and his crew.

That it is buried here is now an undisputed fact, and that it is not on the Cape at the present time my story shall divulge. Sailing, fishing and working, I had passed many delightful weeks, drinking in the invigorating air and gaining flesh and strength every day. Late one afternoon, about the fourth week of my stay, I reached the opening to the bay after whipping a mile or two of the river. My creel was full of beautiful fish, for which I knew the cook was waiting, but, noticing how unusually low was the tide, I strolled along the beach beneath the cliffs and gave myself up to admiration of their peculiarities, accentuated as they were by the kaleidoscopic rays of the evening sun, bursting upon them across acres of placid, reflecting water, broken here and there by the jumping trout. All the mysteries of the domestic economy of crab and lobster were clearly revealed, the only sounds breaking the superb silence being the bark of the stork and the plaintive, excited cry of the graceful harbour gull. Slowly wandering along, I gave no attention to where I was moving and cleared the point by a mile before I was aware that the tide was returning rapidly and would bar my way back.

"The sun had set, leaving the atmosphere one glowing

cauldron of roseate splendour. At the extreme point I found it was impossible to pass without getting wet up to the elbows. There was nothing to do but climb the cliff and work my way along its broken surface. The task was easy at first, but took time, and long before I cleared the point it was evident I should have to stay where I was or climb the perpendicular to the top. The tide was rising over the rocks below, the spray making my foothold slippery and uncertain; but I struggled on and gradually ascended until I arrived at a smooth, flat, perpendicular space without the slightest projection, which extended some five or six feet above my head. This, however, was soon overcome by cutting several niches for my feet about a foot apart, and I rose higher and higher. While digging out the upper one my blade struck against a metal substance and brought to light an old-fashioned iron handle strongly welded to a flat iron plate.

"Fate was kind, I thought: it was the one thing necessary to assist my ascent. It was rusty and deeply encrusted with earth, but it afforded sufficient hold for my purpose, and I clutched it, thinking of it only as a means of deliverance from a wet skin at least. As I did so, the flat block to which it was attached moved and the soil broke away in all directions, revealing a surface about a foot and a half square, confined at the sides by heavy iron bands studded with strong bolts. My surprise was great, but nothing convincingly entered my mind. Its whole appearance denoted great age, the rust and discolouration suggesting many restful years in its novel grave.

"Another wrench to prove if the handle would bear my weight showed me that the rusty bolts were all loose in their rotten sockets, from which a heavy pull would part them, and perhaps hurl me into the roaring sea. Simultaneously with this thought came another, and I realized to what I was clinging. My heart gave a great jump as the stories I had heard rushed through my mind — "Abel's Cape," "Divining rods," "Moonlight diggings," "Kidd's Treasure." Yes, the old-fashioned handle was attached to a wooden chest. Time and moisture had weakened the boards and loosened its bindings, and here it was reserved for me to find.

"I tore away the iron from the rotten wood, and let it fall with heavy splashes into the sea, disclosing the interior of the chest filled with objects that made me giddy with joy. I hardly realized I was standing on almost nothing, but knocked away the dirt above it and clung heavily to its lid while investigating its contents, delicious thoughts flying through me, the like of which until now had not been mine. But let me tell it calmly or I shall be accused of romance and perjury.

"The first things I noticed were several leathern bags at the bottom of the chest, half buried in the shreds and dust. As I clutched one it broke in pieces like an egg-shell and disclosed a heap of golden coins, larger than I had ever owned. There must have been forty of these heaps in all, each containing two hundred pieces. This alone was fortune, but in addition were massive pieces of plate, golden goblets, diamond-studded sword hilts and crucifixes, boxes containing necklaces and bracelets of precious stones and rings; while among the dust and shreds were hundreds of loose pearls, evidently the trimming of some decayed fabric, many of them of great size and beauty, and worth fabulous sums. Long before I realized the value of my find, my head was whirling. Here was wealth a king might envy.

"What should I do with it? I who had slaved all my life from hand to mouth. I would gratify every wish. I would study art and improve my poor profession. I would do some great charitable deed to cover my multitude of sins and hand my name down to posterity. And yet, how to protect it for all this? It must not be left in the cliff. I must get it secretly to a hiding place of my own. I didn't want the Cape overrun with sightseers.

"Hastily I emptied my creel of its silver fish, and filled it with glittering gold. What a frightful weight it was, but what a glorious burden! This all took time, working as I was with one hand. I had quite forgotten where I was, and thought only of Captain Kidd and his generosity to me, when I was brought to the sense of my danger by a wave washing over my left foot and washing away the lower niche on which it rested. My whole weight was on it and the top of the chest. The sudden jerk as I slipped made the lid cave in. It was a miracle that I did not loose my hold. Another wave released my right foot and left me hanging by both hands to the chest's rotten timbers. The waves crept higher, lashing me furiously as though they knew I was desecrating the grave they had guarded so carefully.

"The gulls flew by like lightning, grazing my head with their sharp wings, and piercing my ears with their shrill cries. The wind howled, and the rain began to beat down savagely. The ghosts were indeed out but I was not even nervous. It was right that I should pay something for such a treasure. To gain it by labour and danger seemed only natural. How long, though, could I hold on? To ascend was out of the question. I must hang until the tide turned. But, with the great weight choking me, could I hold till then? All spinal action was prevented by my glorious burden. My arms were becoming cramped, my breath came short, my extremities were chilled by the water. My head was dizzy, and seemed on fire in spite of the wet. Again and again was I drenched by the waves. One, larger than the rest, broke right over my hands, and freed the lid. My grasp relaxed, and I was hurled like a bullet to the bottom of the foaming sea.

"At first it was comparatively easy; the heavy gold held me still, but I had to free myself or drown. The moment I did so, my body was at the mercy of the waves, I shot to the surface and madly tried to swim. Useless. They were punishing me for my presumption, and hurled me about with glee as they washed the precious contents from the chest. Suddenly all was black. My struggles were over, my danger and my fortune alike were forgotten.

"Early the following morning I came to myself, stretched

upon a flat rock, stiff and bruised, my head matted with coagulated blood, the placid waters rippling on the beach yards and yards below me. I was carried home by an early seaweed gatherer, and for two weeks remained in bed, my attendants attributing my story to delirious fancies. No one would believe me. Their jeers, laughs and silly humourings chafed me exceedingly and precluded my recovery. I could think of nothing but my find; and long before I should have left my bed I was on the beach hunting for my golden-lined creel. But nowhere could I find it. Every vestige of the chest, too, had been washed away — only a nearly square hole in the cliff indicating where it had been. For weeks I have searched and delved in the sand, but all to no purpose save the amusement of the islanders. Incredible though it is, my treasure is gone; Kidd's spirit knew how to protect it.

The gentleman named "Flockie," mentioned by Mr. Kent, related another tale of justified murder which we have included. He was also involved with theatre, and penned a story of ghosts and pirates in which he himself was a character. Should we assume the relationship was imaginary?

Lost Baby Lures
Ghost Again and Again

Back in 1864, a Mrs. Pence of the Isle of Wight, wrote of the following event for Mr. Wilfred Ward and Lord Tennyson, and it was sent to the English Society for Psychical Research.

In 1856, Mrs. Pence was taken to a house called Binnestead, located about six miles east of Charlottetown, and believed to be referred to later as the Heartz property. She related it was a good-sized house, and at the back had been considerably extended to allow for extra offices which could only be entered through the inner kitchen, as no wall had been broken down to form a passage or door from upstairs. Thus, she explained, the farming men's sleeping rooms were adjacent to the family and their visitors, even though there was no communicating passageway.

One night, Mrs. Pence's party began hearing strange noises which recurred frequently, and were heard in every part of the house. The rumbling sound, which made the house vibrate, always appeared to be in close proximity to each person who heard it. The more fanciful likened it to the sound of a body being dragged across a floor.

As spring came, shrieks were heard, ghastly sounds that seemed to vary in loudness, as if someone were being chased around the house.

A tree stood just outside the dining room, so close its branches nearly touched a bedroom window, located upstairs near the men's sleeping quarters. Shrieks, sobs, moans, and rambling words, seeming to come from the tree, always ended the tirade.

In February, probably in the year 1857, the inhabitants of the room near the tree were sleeping peacefully, warmed by a fire burning in the grate.

In the small hours of the morning, the women awoke and saw an apparition, so far as Mrs. Pence knew, the first such sighting. A ghostly woman, holding a babe in one arm as she stoked the fire with the other, stooped before the grate. She was a young woman who wore a checked shawl, and looked at them with pleading anxiety showing in her eyes.

In the spring of that same year, Mrs. Pence was herself sleeping in the same room, tending her daughter-in-law who was ill. At the witching hour of midnight, the two were awake for the administration of medicine, when they saw a light under the door. Thinking it to be her charge's father, Mrs. Pence opened the door, only to find a woman, with a babe in her arms, wearing a check shawl. On her face was the same look of entreaty that had been described to Mrs. Pence.

Even though the nocturnal visitor crossed the hall and disappeared through a wall, the ladies were not afraid, not even when Mr. Pence examined the wall and found it solid.

After this occurrence Mrs. Pence went to England, and on her return in 1858, she was told that the screaming had been heard several times, always in the vicinity of the same room near the men's quarters.

One particular male servant, Harry, had frequent visits, but was very close-mouthed about the affair. He was a private individual and would never allow others in his room to watch for the ghostly visitor. His room in the men's quarters was adjacent to that where the sightings had occurred, implying the apparition passed through the solid walls at will.

The following year, Mrs. Pence left the home and the Island itself for an extended time and did not hear any more about the affair until 1877, when she and the local parish priest discussed the Binnestead residence. He had been asked by the wife of the present owner to come and try to dispense with the ghost of a young woman and babe who haunted the house.

Later, when she went to live in Charlottetown, Mrs. Pence came across some curious facts. A number of years before, a man who was described as being uncouth and slovenly of habit, but a capital farmer, had purchased Binnestead from a rich Englishman. It was he who added the back wing to the house.

Two sisters were in this farmer's service, themselves poor and in dire straits. The farmer's immorality was evidenced by baby boys, born to the sisters at about the same time, although little could be learned of circumstances in the house by those who lived nearby. It did seem certain that one sister and one baby disappeared, but no details could be proved.

One must suspect as well that, considering the circumstances in the home, no one cared to venture forward and investigate.

The farm was again sold and the sister, after depositing the baby with her parents, went to the States and never returned. She only told her parents that the boy was her sister's, her own baby being dead.

Harry Newbury, it turned out, was that boy — unknowingly hired to work on the farm where his mother and cousin had died. Harry eventually left, never to return.

The
Shadow of Holland Cove

This accounting is taken from a work, Myths & Legends Beyond Our Borders, *written by Charles M. Skinner, and published by J. B. Lippincott of Philadelphia in 1899.*

"In 1764 came the first white settler to Holland Cove, Prince Edward Island, — surveyor, one Captain Holland, who gave his name to the place where he had set up his habitation. With him presently appeared a woman, of Micmac origin on her mother's side, but her father was a French count, belike, for she was tall, distinguished, and in mind and bearing unlike the majority of half-breeds. Racine was the name whereby she was best known. Of her history the captain's associates knew nothing, or wisely professed to know nothing. During the winter after his arrival the captain was frequently absent on hunting and surveying trips, and on one of these excursions he was gone so long beyond the appointed time that Racine undertook to cross the cove on ice, to see if she might not find some token of him or meet him the sooner. Such, at least, was the supposition. It was an unwise venture, for the ice was infirm, and, falling between two floes, she disappeared. Holland mourned her loss on his return, and attempts were made to find her body, but without avail.

On a still night in the following summer the coxswain of

the captain's party was wakened by a sound of low voices in the sitting-room, and, knowing that all hands had turned in, his curiosity was roused. Lighting a tallow dip, he peered into the room and to his surprise saw Racine. Her position made it seem as if she were seated on the knees of a figure in the captain's easy-chair. The voices were subdued until they were almost whispers, so that the steady drip of water from the woman's clothing could be heard distinctly. At the approach of the coxswain Racine arose and fled past him into the garden, going as silently as possible, yet leaving an odour of sea-damp and a trail of moisture along the floor. There was quite a pool of brine before the chair. To the spectator's surprise, the chair was empty. Had it been vacated while his eyes were on the retreating woman? He stood puzzled, uncertain, and seemed to hear the words, "Why doesn't he come? I must meet him," receding from the open door. Then he heard a splash at the shore. This roused him, and he called up the house, Captain Holland arising with the others. In ten words he told what he had seen, and all hurried to the water, but again nothing was seen or heard. There were the puddled wet, the track of a soaked dress, the open door. Who had been there? With whom met? Still, they think nowadays it was a ghost, and that all who see it will die of drowning. If you disbelieve in spirits and have a faith that you will die in your bed, you may care to watch at Holland Cove on the night of the 14th of July, at the hour when the tide is high.

In 1896, F. Gerald wrote of the Ghost of Holland Cove in the October issue of Canadian Magazine. *He told of going to the cove on a camping expedition with a group of friends and having the tale related by their "genial" host. The party, in good fun, decided to stay awake that night, the date being correct, to see if Racine would pay a visit. One of their number, a young lad called Sam did indeed cry out that he had seen the apparition.*

F. Gerald wrote, "... as soon as he had partly recovered he was plied with questions. The boy's answers the men might believe or not as they liked; but the expression of his eyes was so peculiar that all were struck with it — a far-away, painful, strained look, more as if looking inward that outward. He described what he had seen as a woman's form, tall and clad in sombre garb, stealing away from the mouth of the cellar towards the edge of the cliff, and that he had lost it just as it appeared to be passing over the water; then he cried out and could not look further. There was no volubility in his tale. On him the apparition had left an indelible impression; real or unreal, the outward or mental vision of the boy had photographed on it what he described. Perhaps those who know better than I can explain it all. I leave it to them."

The
Fork in the Graveyard

Author F. H. MacArthur set the scene for the origin of this tale in the collection of folk tales, Folklore of Prince Edward Island. *This particular story is said to have been passed down by word of mouth. It began on a cold day in late October with a fine mist blowing in from the sea. Seated about the pot-bellied stove in the little country store were a group of farmer folk whose talk had turned from problems of the day to current superstitions.*

The tale of Peter MacIntyre is as exciting a story of the supernatural as one is likely to find and, as such, is still repeated by the people of Tracadie who puzzle over the episode to this day.

The spirit, or ghost, of a dead man is said to have committed the dastardly deed of murdering our Peter, a Scottish settler, who arrived in the area on the good ship *Alexander* in 1773.

The scene is set as we described, men relaxing around the warmth of a stove, chatting of mysterious events. When Peter arrived, room was made for him in the warmth, and conversation continued until one Ben Peters mentioned having seen a light in the old French burying place at Scotch Fort. He described a huge ball of fire, dancing across the graves, and lighting up the whole cemetery.

Peter, the newcomer, scoffed at the idea, boasting that such exaggerations would not keep him from walking through any churchyard, even the Scotch Fort one, on that very night.

There were, he claimed, more devils to fear among his mortal companions than in the resting place of the dead.

His boasting, of course, was quickly taken up on, and the challenge thrown out to do more than brag by the comfort of the fire.

"It's all very well to put on a brave front when yer in the company of humans," piped a fellow lounger. "But going to a graveyard that's haunted in the dead of night, and alone, is a horse of another colour. Why, man, you must be clear off your beam to even suggest such a thing let alone go through with it. That old cemetery may be full of dead men's bones, but it's also full of dead men's spirits."

Peter took offense at the remarks, shrugging off superstitious talk as nonsense. The ire was up in his companions who were slighted by his attitude and quickly a bet was made that Peter should go to the old cemetery and plant a hay-fork in a grave, to prove he had been there. Should he succeed a pound of tobacco would be his.

Peter accepted the challenge, and with a jaunty air left the cabin, telling them to have his tobacco ready on the morn, for "I don't expect to be detained by the dead," he said, "I've never knowed dead people to harm anyone."

As it was midnight, all filed from the store. Peter in a long black rain slicker was given the hay-fork and bid on his way to Scotch Fort while the others scuttled for the dry warmth of their own beds.

Come dawn, all were seeking Peter who it seemed had disappeared. His cabin was empty and cold, obviously vacant for some time. More ominous his livestock was bleating with hunger. With the realization that Peter was not to be found came fear, fear for the fate of a man brazen enough to risk defying the very spirits of the dead at the witching hour on a night that seemed to portray the very depths of Hell itself.

The men armed themselves, justifying their actions by expressing a concern about bears in the vicinity, and set out to solve the mystery.

The cemetery was a small clearing in the heart of the forest, reached by means of a narrow footpath, permitting not more than two persons to walk abreast. Every now and then the search party stopped to peer through the branches of the trees, their voices never above a whisper. Finally they were out of the woods and staring in amazement at the sight that met their eyes.

The handle of a hay-fork showed plainly above a grave situated right in the centre of the graveyard. A large black object was curled up on the ground beside it.

Cautiously the party pressed forward, and, as they neared the spot the black object began to take shape. A few more steps and they raised their voices in unison, "Peter! Can't you speak to us"

There was no answer save the echo of their own voices. MacIntyre's body lay across the grave, his face turned toward them. It was a face frozen in agony, a haunted, fear-crazed face that made the living tremble and wish they'd never seen it.

A hand reached out and grabbed the dead man's collar. The hand pulled hard on the collar but the body wouldn't come loose.

A second hand reached out and grasped the fork. It has been driven into the grave with a powerful thrust and right through the tail of Peter MacIntyre's long black coat.

Sea Serpents and Monsters

There are several reports of sea serpents or monsters frequenting the waters of the Island, particularly the south shore. A number of people up around West Point, who are living today, claim to have seen it or know people who have seen it. From the various reports, it is obvious that there has been more than one, and the strange creatures continue to breed in the deep and occasionally visit the shores, probably following schools of fish.

West Point

Around 1980, a sea serpent was reported sighted in the cove between the West Point Lighthouse and the wharf. It was described as being "the length of two fishing boats, that's 60 to 80 feet, long and dark with a head something like a horse." That description tied in with what Carol Livingstone's father saw. Several have said it undulates through the water and that they felt it looking at them.

"My great uncle, Stan MacDonald and Nelson (last name unknown) were out on the water near West Point in a low fishing boat sitting eating lunch. They felt something looking at them. The thing was looking in the boat, the head would come about three feet out of the water. It was not in the least bit threatening. It was up out of the water with its head raised out." Carol Livingstone.

Little Pond

"**M**any years ago a man from Little Pond went shooting. He built a blind out of seaweed, sticks, bushes. The ducks would come in so far and then fly out again before he could get a shot at them so he knew something was scaring them away. He decided to investigate and raised his head to peer over the blind.

"A huge snake like head poked out from the weeds around the shore. He aimed and fired quickly at the monstrous head and killed it. However the apparition began to thrash about in its last agony and the man realized how large the creature really was. He immediately took flight, dropped his gun, and raced to a nearby neighbour's. The neighbours could hardly understand what had happened since he was almost incoherent with fright. They accompanied him back to find the carcass and discovered it to be 14 feet long. They attached a wire to it and pullet it up. It was estimated to weigh close to 300 pounds. It was felt that this monster must have come from the sea." *Those Were The Days — A History of the North Side of the Boughton River.*

Miminegash

"**I**t was August 16, 1879 and Matthew MacDonald and James Doyle were hauling their trawls when they "observed an unusual commotion on the water near them." Suddenly the line MacDonald was hauling was jolted violently and torn through his hands, and 'a huge form arose from the sea a full 20 feet out of the water.'

"The pair set all sail to get the boat away from there with all possible speed, but the monster of the deep gave chase. And what a monster it was. The pair described the fish as a sort of snake, striped yellow and white, with a mouth as large as the open end of a puncheon, 'and each time it raised out of the water it uttered a roar like the bellowing of a bull.'

"MacDonald tried tossing hake (a type of fish) to the monster from the load in the boat, in an attempt to pacify it, but the thing greedily devoured the hake and kept coming.

"MacDonald appeared to have been doing most of the work with the pursuing monster, and he fashioned a weapon from a long knife which he fastened securely to the end of an oar blade. When the pursuer closed the gap and came close to the boat, he rammed the monster's eye, driving the knife clear to the handle or end of the oar blade. The knife broke in the wound.

'With a roar of pain the monster sank out of sight, the old story relates,' reddening the water around with its blood.'

"Doyle who was watching the performance said he 'counted 12 sharp fins on it, each surmounted with a sort of horn,' and both men said the fish was 200 feet long.

"Next day while repairing their broken line they took from one of the hooks a large tuft of yellow hair, attached to a piece of skin resembling pigskin. The two men worked for E. G. Fuller and, the story said, this tuft of hair and skin, 'could be seen at his establishment.'

"An incredible yarn for sure, yet it was told as a true story, with the tuft of hair and skin to prove it."

Taken from a newspaper clipping which is part of the Leard Collection of the Public Archives of P.E.I. The details were said to have been found originally with tales from *Old Charlottetown and P.E.I.*

Romantic Link
Made on Hallowe'en

One E. F. Moyse related this tale, saying that while not a unique story, it was still interesting enough to attract the notice of the American Branch of the Society for Psychical Research in the late 1800s.

It was Hallowe'en, and around a merry fireside in Bedeque, upward of forty years ago (making it the mid 1800s), were being related some of the wonderful things performed by one or other of the family on previous anniversaries of that occasion, when the unseen powers are said to have unusual sway. Among the many remarkable possibilities that might be taken advantage of on that night by those who were bold enough to undertake them, was a way by which a person might find out who was to be his or her life partner. An ambition seized one of the daughters of the family to make a test of these alleged spiritualistic powers that very night. Accordingly, when all was quiet, about "the witching hour of midnight," Miss R--- proceeded to a secluded up-stair room, and, by the flickering light of a candle, she carried out the formula of combing her hair before a mirror, at the same time eating an apple.

We should almost expect great nervousness on her part at this point when she would remember that if a coffin appeared over her shoulder, instead of the image of her future husband, it would mean that she could not live another year. This, of course, had been proven to be terribly true, according to the testimony of others; and, no doubt, this young lady's mind was not free from the fear that the dreaded coffin might appear. It must have been a keen test of her courage. Everything was deathly quiet, the comb silently sweeping through her waving hair, when suddenly she beheld a man peering over her shoulder in the mirror. The exact features, and even the hat which the apparition wore, were stamped indelibly on her mind in an instant. Fright took possession of her, and she fled hysterically from the room.

The incident was almost forgotten till late in the autumn when one day she met, at a friend's house, a gentleman whose face so forcibly brought to her mind the weird experience of Hallowe'en that she was almost prostrated again. The stranger's face seemed the exact duplicate of the apparition. This gentleman, whom we shall call Mr. C---, had left his home some fifty or sixty miles away and come to Bedeque in quest of a farm. Previous to this he had not the slightest knowledge of, or acquaintance with, Miss R---; she was, likewise, ignorant of his existence. Mr. C--- was successful in obtaining land, and it was only a short while till he and Miss R--- were married and comfortably settled in their new home.

There are two sides to every story, and this is no exception. Mr. C---'s experience, in connection with the events as narrated, gives the whole matter a more decided colouring.

We go back with Mr. C--- to his former home on that same Hallowe'en, and find that he, as well as the rest of the family, had retired as usual; but, about midnight, by some means or other, they became aware that there was something wrong with the above-mentioned member of the family. We have not at our disposal the particulars regarding his exact condition at this time; but he seemed to be in an unconscious state, which was thought sufficiently alarming to warrant the attendance of a physician. One was summoned at once, but treatment was to no avail, and he was forced to confess that he did not understand the case. Mr. C--- was taken from his bed by a couple of his brothers and, supporting him on either side, they walked him about the floor; finally, placing a hat on his head, they took him out into the open night air to see if its freshness would revive him. All efforts, however, failed to arouse him from his mysterious and profound sleep, and he was again placed in bed. Soon afterwards, he regained himself and passed into a sleep, from which he awoke in the morning quite ignorant of what had taken place.

The matter was not mentioned to him in the morning; but, when his father insisted that he should take a rest that day, his curiosity was greatly aroused, for such unusual consideration, while in the best of health, he certainly thought demanded an explanation. The trance-like condition he had passed through on the previous night was described to him, but he had no recollection of it whatever.

More facts might be gathered as to the exact symptoms exhibited by Mr. C--- during his trance, but perhaps we have sufficient for the purpose.

Dare we suggest, in this enlightened age, that Mr. C---'s spirit took leave of his body and, in some way, became visible to Miss R--- in the mirror? On the other hand, considering how limited is our knowledge of things spiritual, dare we deny that such a thing is possible?

No one, who ever knew Mr. and Mrs. C---, doubted their veracity; and we tell the story, in substance, as often related by them. We are, then, left to conjecture: (1) Was the apparition wholly the result of expectancy? (2) Was the similarity between the face in the mirror and the stranger's face the result of imagination? (3) Was the apparent connection between the two experiences on that Hallowe'en a mere coincidence? If not, there must be a means by which an influence is exerted by one mind upon another, other than through the recognized sensory channels.

The
Ghost of Barlow Road

Tales of the ghostly lady and evil spirits, who frequented the area near Brenan's Tavern on Barlow Road between Ellerslie and Lot 11, must be questioned; for many reportings of sightings followed an evening of revelry and heavy drinking at the tavern. There were, however, enough accountings to give some credence to the existence of the ghost, although most have her simply standing erect at the side of the road waiting, as she told one passerby, for "her Albert." The region was spooky in those days, for the Barlow Road between Ellerslie and Lot 11 passed through barrens known locally as the "blueberry plains" or "the barrens," an area wracked by fire which lay wasted for a century and a half. The area did not attract residents, so it took on a particularly lonely atmosphere.

F. H. MacArthur wrote of an incident involving one Ben Horne, an older fellow who had carried a bag of flour to the tavern where he sold it, and then tipped back a goodly few before leaving for the long walk home to Port Hill. Other sightings of the Lady Ghost of Barlow Road were recorded in The Prince Edward Island Magazine.

About midpoint between the tavern and Port Hill, close to Grant's Creek, stood a stately pine, aged and scarred by its battle with the elements, for survival in this bleak place. This "Halfway Tree" was said to be where evil lurked. In fact some believed that spirits lived in the tree. Among them was the legendary "Ghost Lady of Barlow Road."

After an afternoon at the tavern, Ben started out for home. The sun was high in the sky, and the time estimated at 4:30 p.m. — too early in the day for the normal appearance of what was to follow.

As he neared Grant's Creek, Ben was surprised to see a snake fence across the road. Being of reasonable intelligence, he realized that something was not right, and claimed afterward that he thought it might be the spirits he had heard others speak of. Even so, home he had to go, so he began to climb the fence.

Suddenly a woman's piercing scream rent the air causing the "very hair on his head to stand up like the bristling mane of an angry dog." When Ben realized the Ghost Lady was near the fence, he collapsed and fell sprawling to the ground.

The story goes that Ben recovered his wits and jumped to his feet, looking for the frightful apparition. Instead of the ghostly lady, the fence poles righted themselves to stand on end and, turning into soldiers, began to march down the road in formation, as might be expected of soldiers of the day. Ben still had enough about him to count, and count he did. But even as he did, the thirty marching men turned into lumbering giants, each wearing a cap, cloak, and shoes.

Now the Ghostly Lady appeared, driving the giants towards the hapless Ben, using a bull whip to force them on. He knew she was the ghost by her resemblance to the descriptions of men before him — tall, wearing a snowy white robe that went right to the ground, and missing her left arm.

Their pace was slow, but as they methodically advanced towards him, poor old Ben suffered some anxious moments before the procession turned off the road, marched to the "Halfway Tree," and vanished.

Tree, tavern, and the ghostly lady have gone, but Grant's Creek still runs true and the legend lives on.

Naked Nathan

At a certain phase in the history of the Island, many strong-bodied men left to work the woods in Maine. Good money could be made in a winter there, enough to warrant leaving family and friends behind. The camps paid as much as fifteen dollars per month, with room and board supplied. When work ended each spring, most of the men returned to the Island, pockets stuffed with money. What a temptation for those who found it easier to take than toil! One also wonders if many of those young men spent more on pleasures than they should, and made up tales of being set upon to account for less than the expected wealth they were to bring home. One tale that causes such pondering is that of Nathan Clark.

Teen-age Nathan Clark was a tall broad-shouldered fellow whose strength had proved him proficient with the axe. When warm weather closed the Maine logging operation where he had found winter employment, Nathan sewed his fortune — said to be one hundred dollars — in his undershirt, and started for home in Riverton.

Nathan had done well in the woods. He also had with him travelling money, a new suit, and his prized family heirloom, a silver watch chain inherited from his father. His journey to the Island was fairly uneventful; he arrived weary, but happy at the thought of the coming reunion with family and friends.

Nathan had borrowed a horse and buggy from a friend, and with less than a day's journey left, was pleased with life. He was heard singing by those he passed. Darkness descended just as he arrived at the crest of the hill down to Cran's Brook; it was here that trouble began.

The mare stopped dead in her tracks and could not be coaxed forward, even when Nathan got down from the buggy and tried to force her. Suddenly five witches burst from the woods, a sinister laugh the only warning of their presence.

Terrified, Nathan ran, trying to get across the creek and pull up the board of the bridge to stop the witches in their tracks (apparently everyone knew that witches could not cross water). He was not fast enough.

Caught, he was dragged back and robbed of all his prized possessions including his clothes. A humiliated Nathan was left with a sore, aching body from the abuse railed upon him, and naught else.

Fairy Rings

An Irish legend tells of fairies, brought from the old country in the braided manes and tails of horses. These fairies quickly settled to life on the Island.

Although seldom seen, evidence of their presence was obvious by the edges of the woods, where "fairy rings" of mushrooms grew.

Anyone who saw one of these fairy rings had to act quickly to ward off a spell that would cause them to go back to the old country. The spell was broken by "doing something — putting something away."

The question is whether the superstition had a factual base, or was one invented by frustrated folks, facing the practicality of needing a way to get people to do things.

Tignish

Some areas are steeped in fascinating legends and ghost stories. The very place itself seems to lure the occurrence of supernatural events. Among the ghostly tales coming from residents of the area is the one that on August 15th of each year the phantom ship, mentioned in detail elsewhere, will be sighted. For some reason, the burning ghost ship repeatedly visits the area on that date. A few more tales follow that tell of the rich tradition of the area.

Ghost of St. Simon and St. Jude

The landscape of Tignish and area has been dominated by the Gothic spire of the Roman Catholic Church of St. Simon and St. Jude since its completion in 1860. Up to three miles distant, the spire can be seen with the naked eye, towering over all other structures.

The beautiful church was the largest on the Island for many years. Designed by a famous New York architect and built by local artisans of locally-made brick, it presides over a community that has changed little over the years.

It seems only right and true that such a proud structure

should have a resident ghost to strike terror into the hearts of the less pious members of the congregation.

The best time to hear the old fellow clanking his chains is around three in the afternoon, when the ghost of a man who committed murder long, long ago, visits the altar.

The fellow, you see, was never brought to justice, although everyone around Tignish knew he was guilty. Unpunished in his mortal life, he was condemned after death to go up to the high altar in chains each day in mid-afternoon.

I have never had the misfortune of hearing the clanking chains, and can't say I miss the opportunity of making the acquaintance of the ghost of St. Simon and St. Jude.

Haw Bush Treasure

This tale takes place closer to North Cape than Tignish. Buried treasure has been attracting adventurous diggers for many a year, but so far no one has admitted to discovering the Haw Bush Treasure.

As in other treasure episodes, it is necessary to dig in complete silence. One word alerts the spirits protecting the trove, and your chances have flown like an owl in the night.

Another similarity between this and other supposed treasures is that a mysterious, bone-chilling event occurs which causes diggers to panic and speak.

A loud, frightening sound is heard once digging starts. It's usually described as a horse and carriage galloping, as if a runaway. The sound comes from a direction where no such noise should be heard. Surprised diggers utter an oath, a startled gasp, or even a warning, and once that happens all chance of finding the treasure is gone.

It is said that it will take a deaf man to break the spirits' hold and claim the treasure of Haw Bush.

Chest on a Reef
A Lure to the Phantom Ship

E lsewhere in this book, we tell you of the Phantom Ship
of Northumberland Strait, the extraordinary phenomenon of a burning, three-masted schooner.

At North Cape, the ship has been sighted on a regular
basis just off the reef. It almost always is seen on August
15th, an extraordinary sight, with flames engulfing the ship.
No one knows why it appears so often on that date, why it
burns but never sinks, or even why it has come to North
Cape.

One possible reason is a treasure chest, that apparently
can be seen at very low tide, way out on the long reef that
runs east from the Cape. Incidentally, this reef is reputed to
be one of the longest in the world, and surely brought more
than one ship to her doom.

Why the ship visits on a specific day of the year is a total
mystery, unless perhaps that is the day of a sinking or battle
which caused the chest of treasure to be lost on the reef.

Blumphey's Ghost
At Tignish Run

O ur final Tignish tale comes from Tignish Run, where
one Sunday evening in May, three fishermen joined
their friends at Myrick's bunkhouse for a wee bit of relaxa-
tion before the coming week of lobster fishing. It was the
custom for men from around the area to bunk at Myrick's
while working from the Run.

Their journey took them along a sandy road that followed the shores of MacLeod's Pond, known today as Little
Tignish River, and it was natural that conversation turned
to fishing, the catch, and what was in store for the coming week.

When a fourth man joined the party, they hailed him with the jaunty hail used to greet all friends and neighbours. The silent response caused all three to look at their new comrade. He looked to be one of their own type of man, and yet shivers ran up and down spines, and a sense of deep foreboding was experienced.

The silence of the evening set an eerie atmosphere. Add to it the failure of the newcomer to speak, and you have three very unhappy fishermen. As they walked on, the silence became more and more oppressive, until suddenly the fourth man disappeared.

With his disappearance, the trio began to question the stranger's presence, even questioning each other for not finding out more about him. One claimed to have reached out to touch the mystery man's jacket, only to encounter nothing but air.

Not understanding what was going on, and not being inclined to want to find out, they "got out of there" and shortly were back in the bunkhouse, where co-workers were chatting and enjoying a smoke.

Their agitated manner and faces as white as sheets were noticeable to the others, even though they denied anything being wrong.

One of the company twigged. "You've seen Blumphey," he cried, and went on to explain that a ghost was known to walk the shore by MacLeod's Pond. It is thought to be an Irishman who did not settle well on the Island, a fellow who was very lonely and inclined to brood.

He was found one day, hanging from the rafters of a shed. Because of laws prohibiting suicides from burial in a churchyard, his body was placed in a shallow grave on the banks of MacLeod's Pond.

Years later the bank caved in and, in the usual manner of such stories, Blumphey's body went missing. Ever since, the ghost has been reported along the road where he used to spend hours pacing, and probably longing for places or persons left in Ireland.

The newcomers had not, of course, heard of Blumphey, and didn't really want to make further acquaintance. In the discussion that their sighting aroused, it was determined that he always appeared in the early evening in the same location, and never caused any more harm that a few moments of fear.

A couple of years later, a smelt fisherman was waiting for his partner below the pond. He had gone ahead out on their dory, but kept looking shoreward until finally he saw him, and began to row ashore to pick him up. As he shouted to the form standing just above the pebbly beach, he realized it neither moved nor spoke and was slowly fading away. Blumphey had been spotted again, and again drove man from his regular pursuits to flee for safer quarters.

Blumphey seems to have found his peace around 1925, for there are no documented reports of his presence since then, although there were many prior to that time. The road is still there, changed little by progress. The cemetery, too, can be found, although it is decayed by time and overgrown by trees.

The Ghostly
Miller of Clyde River

I first heard about the ghostly Good Samaritan of Scott's Mill when visiting one of the most popular newspaper columnists of her era, the author of "Ellen's Diary." "Ellen's Diary" ended before my sojourn at the Guardian *in Charlottetown, yet people often asked about the column and its author. That interest led me to interview the retired writer in her home for a feature article. That was when I first heard of the "Ghostly Miller of Scott's Mill."*

The remains of the old grist mill are located near her home and, as we chatted in the garden, she mentioned the strange tale, just one of the odd events that happened when John Scott and his sons owned and operated the mill.

In those days the mill was popular with farmers over a wide area, because the miller took pride in turning out the highest quality flour in Queen's County. The family were hard-working and proud of the work done at the mill.

When illness beset the family, John Scott worried about his customers almost as much as about his fevered wife and children. Fate, as is her usual wont, had laid the family ill at a time when there was much wheat to be ground. They could ill afford time to lie abed, yet were unable to do the heavy work.

Scott must have wondered if his mind was playing tricks when he suddenly heard the mill groan to life. Concerned that someone was meddling with his machinery, Scott threw on outer garments and hurried down a steep incline to the mill.

Presumably lit by intruders, a lighted lantern, hanging outside the entrance, marked his way. Angered by the trespass, and by being forced out into the night air when ill, he armed himself with a sturdy stick.

As he drew near the mill, it seemed to be almost throbbing with life, as the machinery turned and a fine cloud of dust hung in the air, wafting through the beams of light thrown by the lantern.

Scott stepped across the flume and strode into the mill.

Put yourself in the man's shoes. Here he was expecting to find intruders doing harm in the source of his family's livelihood. Ready to defend himself against the unknown, he was thus stopped in his tracks by the sight that met his eyes.

He was met by the totally unexpected. Everything was running as well as if his own hands were tending the machinery. The mill was running, hopper filled, bags in place to catch the flour; there was naught he could do to improve the operation. Yet all was not as it should be. A stranger's footsteps could be heard; they clumped on the stairs. Scott watched an unknown figure of a man descend through the light of the lantern, hung in the centre of the mill. Things became even more* puzzling when the actions of the stranger, checking the working of the mill, the flow of the grain, marked him as an experienced miller.

Suddenly, before Scott had managed to speak to his nocturnal visitor, a door banged, the lanterns were snuffed, and the mill stopped grinding, as if some modern day switch had been thrown.

Silence prevailed.

Being near the lantern, Scott struck a match and restored light, expecting to greet the stranger. But all was silent — Scott was alone. No footsteps or opening doors had signalled his leaving, yet the stranger was not to be found — anywhere.

On asking around, Scott never could find an identity for the ghostly miller. It was as if he did not exist, at least in the form of a living human.

That he had been in the mill, Scott was certain, for three bags of ground flour bore testimony to his presence.

Those bags of flour were sorely needed by the ill miller and his family. One wonders if he regretted disturbing the ghostly visitor before a full night's work had been done.

The Smugglers of Holland Cove

F. Gerald had another tale to tell of Holland Cove. He and a "merry party" camped at the Cove during the summer of 1896 with five tents supplying accommodation, and a nearby house, a spot for eating and occasional dancing. They had, he said, "an occasional incident" and described the following as one of them.

This tale is but one of thousands, concerning the days of rum runners bringing illegal goods to the Island during prohibition. Many fortunes were made by smugglers, and incredible links existed among sailors of the Gulf and the hoodlums of the United States. We will not go into the matter in great detail, for the subject is well documented by a research/writing team from Tyne Valley, P.E.I., Dr. and Mrs. Geoff Robinson. But this tale is worthy of relating:

"On the fourteenth of August one or two of the members of our party remarked upon the appearance of two schooners which lay out about two miles in the offing for some days without apparent reason. That day the wind had shifted pretty well all round the compass, but no sails had been set to the breeze, nor was there any sign of busy life on board either vessel.

The afternoon set in cloudy, giving the promise of a dark night. It was noticed that shortly before sunset one of the schooners had hauled off from her companion and had anchored considerably nearer the shore.

As we sat round the camp fire that evening comment was freely made as to what was detaining these vessels. It was laughingly suggested "perhaps they are smugglers," but no one seriously entertained the thought.

At midnight it was as dark as "Erebus," and the camp lay in apparent peaceful slumber undisturbed by thoughts of lawlessness; the gentle breeze off shore being only just sufficient to cool the air. In one tent, however, there were three young ladies wide awake, aged respectively — I may tell their ages in the strictest confidence — sixteen, eighteen, and twenty; nameless however they must remain, as I obtained all my information only after making the most solemn promise of secrecy.

"I believe they are smugglers," said the youngest girl, just loud enough for her two companions to hear. "Listen," again said the girl, "what is that?"

"Oars," said both the other ladies in an excited whisper. They all listened for a moment and the measured sound of muffled oars was faintly but distinctly audible.

The three girls rose from their cots and stood in the door of the tent. Each had hastily wrapped herself in a light white dressing gown. The older one now said, "Girls, this is nonsense, it is only someone landing in the cove," but the tremor in her voice belied this calm assurance of prosaic incident.

"I am going to see, anyway," broke forth number two, the "Jean D'Arc" of the party, as she tossed her flowing tresses over her shoulders. Her wilful, buoyant nature was stirred with the thought of a real adventure.

"If one of you girls stir out from this tent I'll light the lamp and rouse the camp," was the quick reply of the elder girl.

"Do," replied the former speaker with ill concealed raillery in her tone "and get our dear old papas and mammas and all our male guardians in a mad rush to the beach 'en deshabille' to see your — farmer's boy returning from town. Well, I would not like to be in your shoes when they get back, that's all," and the girl laughed as she thought of the scene.

What conversation followed I was not told. It ended in the older one being persuaded to go with her two companions "just to the brow of the hill" overlooking the beach, where a few spruce bushes offered a safe observation point; from whence could be seen what was being enacted on the shore, tragedy or comedy.

Silently the three white robed figures stole with unshod feet towards the sheltering trees, two at least of them bubbling over with excitement. No sound from their little feet disturbed the slumbering camp, and in a very few moments they had traversed the one hundred yards which brought them to the suggested lookout. Here they heard distinctly the sound of oars, and the murmuring of voices, but it was too dark to see anything on the beach now some eighty yards below them; and listen they ever so intently they could hear nothing to enable them to determine the character of the midnight boatmen, but to the quick ear of "Jean" there were the sounds of many voices, hushed voices, and voices of command.

Some fifty yards further down the gradual slope to the shore was another thick clump of bushes, where the eager, adventurous spirit of the two younger girls urged a further advance. No use now the objections urged by their companion; indeed, they were feebly pressed, for interest in their quest had quickened her pulse also, and fear of failure was then greater than any dread of discovery.

No darker night ever, I think, spread its pall over our northern clime than sheltered our fair night-rovers in their last steal to within a few yards of the edge of the beach, where grew the sheltering trees under whose cover the trust was to be learned.

Once there they were not long in doubt. They could see obscurely, but unmistakably, three boats, two on the shore and one just landing, and the dim but discernible forms of many men busy unloading the two boats and carrying bales and barrels into the wooded recesses of the cove.

"Smugglers," whispered "Jean," as after a moment's observation the girls drew closer together behind the bush. "There are twenty men at work at least. Oh! what fun, what shall we do?"

"Quick boys, here's the last load," said a low voice close to where the crouching, and now thoroughly startled girls lay hidden.

Not twenty yards from them stood the man who had just spoken, who continued half speaking to himself: "Never a cleaner job done for years right under the nose of Her Majesty's Dominion cutters, and of his mightiness the Commodore of the Canadian Fleet! Bah! it would never do for his men to soil their new toggery just purchased in the Minister's constituency in a rough and tumble with my fellows. I don't want to meet the Commodore though, he shuts his jaw with a snap that means 'to Hell or Connaught' in a fight or I'm mistaken."

"Gently there, you lubber" broke in on the reverie, "do you want," he said, angrily, " to wake up yon sleepers and have them out at our heels like barking curs?"

As he said this, he turned to look up the decline towards the camp. His quick eye must have caught the glint of something, where, almost benumbed with fear, crouched our three little maidens bold. Without a word he walked quickly the few steps which separated them from him. Hardly a moment elapsed when the girls perceived him standing close beside them, and between them and the tents.

"You are out late to-night young ladies," he observed quietly, as the three of them, now realizing their position, stood erect. There was an unmistabable meaning and imputation in his tone of voice.

"Let us pass, sir," replied the elder girl as she and her companions moved to leave their hiding place.

"Hardly just now ladies," answered the man in grim humour, "the men out there" he added, speaking now with quiet intensity "not to speak of myself, have too much at stake to give up without" — he hesitated — "well, say a struggle, that cargo. You have seen too much to be free to work us harm, and God knows I don't want to be forced to meet the men in your camp." Then altering his voice, he continued. "Your presence here is unfortunate, but remain quiet and no harm shall happen to you."

As the speaker stood facing the girls, his manner was gentlemanly and respectful, and that of one accustomed to command. As dimly seen by them in the darkness he was no ordinary, south sea-captain.

"We knew not of your lawless work when we came here" answered the girl, calmly, "and a call from me will quickly rouse the camp when we will need no further protection."

"Perhaps," he answered, "but you came down that slope very quietly, ladies. No one could have come down openly without my seeing them. My eye is keen and ear sharp, and I stood there to watch your camp as well as to direct the landing."

Some of those employed on the shore now missing their superior, and hearing the low voices, came up close to the speakers. "Back to your work men and be quick," was his short, decisive order as soon as he perceived their presence, "I am your surety against harm here."

Gruesome mutterings came from the men as they withdrew and the girls perceived clearly their unpleasant position.

"We are no spies or tell-tales," now broke in 'Jean d'Arc'; and as the man looked in the face of the bright, handsome girl he saw she spoke the truth, or believed he saw, as is the way with all our poor weak sex when Eve's grand-daughter is pretty. He answered smilingly, "I believe that, only possibly a little curious," After a moment's pause he added, "if you promise me on your word of honour to say nothing of what you have seen you are free now to return. What say you to that, ladies? I will take the risk. I like not to keep you in such company, — and so clad," he added hesitatingly.

Quick to decide and seeing that their curiousity had brought them into their present predicament, the way of escape from which appeared neither clear nor extremely pleasant, the elder girl answered at once "we promise."

Bowing low the man stepped aside and said "thank you, ladies, I accept your promise. Good night, and may I say before you go how thankful I am that I discovered your presence. Rough men when caught at this work are not apt to be particularly courteous even to ladies."

"Good night" answered the three girls, and "thank you," added the elder one, who felt that on her shoulders would have rested the blame had aught happened to her companions, and something in the manner of the man seemed to demand recognition of equality; such free trustfulness at any rate deserved at least a simple "thank you."

Once at the tent again the trio stood for a moment looking at one another in breathless silence. What a volume passed without utterance in that short moment! Quickly they crept back into their beds. No light was lit. In excited whispers they discussed their adventure. What might have happened!! 'Jean,' shaking with smothered laughter, whispered across the small space which separated them in the tent, "Oh, I'll never get over it, never! never! The look of our dear old chaperon when she said 'we promise,' posing as a Grand Duchess while trying to hide her toes in the grass. He saw them all right. Oh my, Oh my!" and she shook with laughter.

"Did you hear him laugh when we all went scooting up the hill like white robed angels on the flit? I did, I tell you, and shook my fist at him in return."

"Kissed your hand, you mean," said number three.

"I did not," sharply retorted 'Jean.' "Oh, but you, with your curl papers all hanging loose and hair like a live mop, you looked too beautiful for anything; YOUR hands were too busy holding on to curl papers to do anything so naughty, I suppose." And then she turned to the older girl. "Oh my dear, I'll never forget you, you looked just like 'She' when she stood before her lover in the transformation scene. What symmetry of form! What transparency of costume! old 'penny-a-linner' — the yarn and two thousand for your photograph." ... "I wonder did the captain think we had on our bathing dresses, or that ours was the usual summer NEGLIGE costume of the camp?" ... "What do you think they had, silks or satins or brandy or what? Oh if I only had one little genuine smuggled something as a keepsake from our pirate bold!"

"Hush you goose and go to sleep" here interrupted the eldest, whose desire now was that no noise should disturb the occupants of the other tents.

But "sixteen" and "eighteen" were not so easily suppressed. Well into the night did the two exchange whispered reminiscences. The sound of creaking cordage at length made them stop and listen. The vessels were evidently getting under weigh; all was over, not much fear of trouble now.

"Girls, for the last time I say go to sleep and remember your promise." "We will," answered both the younger girls together, and 'Jean' continued. "You've been a dear old thing and we'll not say another word, and we'll be as mum as mice."

The elder girl had possibly two or three good reasons for reminding them of the promise of secrecy she had made on their behalf. She knew how hard it would be for them to keep bottled up at their age; and perhaps she thought that at her age it would be as well that the adventure should not be detailed with embellishments by the long-tongued gossips of her own sex.

I'll tell you how long they kept it. When the afternoon papers came out the next evening, noticing the following paragraph I read it aloud:

DARING ACT. — The Dominion Cruiser ... arrived this morning. She brought the news that two schooners known to have left St. Pierre, with full cargoes of liquors and some French fabrics, without clearance paper, had safely landed their valuable cargoes somewhere on the southern coast of this Province. The captain further reports that from private instructions received, he had followed in the wake of these vessels for some days hoping to make a seizure, but that unfortunately he had lost sight of them in the recent gale in the Gulf. Seeing them this morning off St. Peter's Island, he had overhauled and searched them, only to find them as clean of everything as a well-picked herring bone. There being nothing to authorize their detention, he was obliged to release them. He believes however, that under cover of the darkness of last night — a particularly dark one — they landed their cargoes not far from the Island named. We trust the revenue officers will make diligent search for these smuggled goods. If the cargoes are only one half as valuable as reported, this is one of the boldest smuggling feats on record in recent years."

"Whew!" exclaimed an old paterfamilias always extremely knowledgeable after the event. "What about our two schooners now? I told you I thought they were on for something, and there was no sign of them this morning."

I caught a startled look in 'Jean's' face as I glanced round after reading. Watching for an explanation I soon perceived what looked like one. For a second after I saw a look of intelligence flash to and from the eyes of three of our young ladies, and as I caught the eye of the youngest with an inquiring look on my face, hers flushed crimson. "Ho! ho! young lady," thought I, "you know something or I'm mistaken."

I spent two days pumping and ferreting and all I got for my pains was that I saw I was plainly shunned by all three.

In the evening however the eldest of them joined me where I was smoking a lone cigar and said "You are making it unpleasant for Miss _____, her friend, and myself. You do not wish to do so, I know. You think we have something we desire to keep secret. We have. Please respect our wish. If you do three years hence I will tell you everything."

"Make it two" I said eagerly, for I saw 'copy' genuine original stuff in her eye.

"I said three," she answered; and last week she kept her promise.

I have told you this story as she told it to me. I believe it is all true, but gentle reader, you can accept as absolute, bald fact just as much as you please. Any doubting Thomas may possibly be able otherwise to account for the parcel addressed to 'Jean' in her true name, which she received in the fall of 1896. It had no other address upon it. Where you would expect to see the sender's name there was only a date written clearly "August fourteenth." The parcel made up into a handsome silk dress.

I have a theory and so has 'Jean.'

F. Gerald

A Phenomenon
of a Battle at Sea

This account again comes from The Prince Edward Island Magazine, *published at the turn of the century. It was written by one O.L.M. who said that, "A great many may not give credence to this story, owing to a sailor relating it, as they are often noted for stretching a yarn at the same time they spin it, but the writer can vouch that all contained in the foregoing is true, as the sailor solemly swore to it. The narrator of the phenomenon makes no secret of it, and will be quite pleased to have an interview with anyone for ascertaining more particulars regarding the strange sight. The writer has, therefore, given a short account of the event, trusting that some reader may give an explanation of these signs in the heavens."*

> *At times he sees the sky-blue dog*
> *Tackle the pale-green cat*
> *While fiery serpents sizzle round*
> *As umpires of the spat;*
> *And purple horses shod with fire*
> *Are climbing lofty trees*
> *And fanning with their scarlet tails*
> *The circumambient breeze.*
>
> — *Skiffling's Prize Temperance Poem*

"This is a tale of an experience that befell a friend of mine, a truthful sailorman who is in no wise descended from the Ancient Mariner, and has never read the Vision of Mirza. If any of the readers of THE PRINCE EDWARD ISLAND MAGAZINE doubt the truth of this story, I can give, as guarantee, the oath of the man with the dyed goatee, who saw the schooner on which the sailorman had the experience. I will relate it as nearly as possible in the graphic style in which my friend communicated it to me':—

"On the 29th of July last we were anchored off Sydney Harbour, C. B. Rain had fallen early in the morning, but towards noon the weather changed to fine and the wind died away, so at our anchorage we had to stay for the rest of the day.

"Shortly after twelve o'clock we had finished dinner, and to while away the time I went up on deck, and stretched myself on the hatch preparatory to enjoying a "good smoke".

"I composed myself for enjoyment. Before me stretched the calm waters of the harbor, bounded by the Cape Breton hills, save where the gap betrayed the outlet to the ocean. I had hardly time to survey the view before me when I gazed upward, as though compelled, and, almost immediately, in the sky above, I beheld the most wonderful and beautiful phenomenon I have ever witnessed.

"A cloud appeared to be scarcely a quarter of a mile away, and in it were all the animals, birds, and reptiles, that cover the earth. There were horses, cattle, sheep, pigs, lions, tigers, bears, wolves, dogs, cats and numerous other animals which I cannot name.

"Some of the birds and reptiles proved very strange to me; more so as I have spent the greater part of my life upon the sea and therefore am not much acquainted with the different species I saw. I thought at first the grand sight was all imagination, but to prove the contrary I called the crew to behold the sight.

"All hand were soon on deck looking at the cloud, admiring, in various ways, its grandeur and beauty. No description can give any idea of the strangeness, splendor and real sublimity of the sight. The Captain on beholding it said that it resembled the account given of the opening of the ark.

"After a short time the cloud passed off to the east but was replaced by one which contained a greater marvel. This was a regiment of soldiers marching, and singing the following as they marched:—

'Hurrah! Hurrah! for France!
Hurrah! Hurrah! for France!

"We could hear it quite plainly, the cloud was moving about, and was nearer us than the other one had been. The Frenchmen gave way to another regiment of soldiers and these sang: —

'Hurrah! Hurrah! for England!
Hurrah! Hurrah! for England!
Hurrah! Hurrah! for England!
And Ireland, too!'

"As this regiment passed along another appeared and these sang: —

'Hurrah! Hurrah! for England!
Hurrah! Hurrah! for England!
Hurrah! Hurrah! for England!
And Bonnie Scotland, too!'

"As this regiment also passed along another appeared and these sang: —

'Hurrah! Hurrah! for England!
Hurrah! Hurrah! for England!
Hurrah! Hurrah! for England!
And the United States, too!'

"Numerous other regiments passed along singing also, —

as we could only understand English we could not tell what country they represented.

"The cloud now changed into a battlefield with its horses, guns and soldiers, and a battle soon began. Each body of soldiers was dressed according to the custom of the country they hailed from. As we were all Scotsmen on board we took great interest in the Scotch regiment, the men of which were dressed in kilts, and were headed by a band of pipers.

"When the battle began we could not tell one army from another, but could see men fall on every side. At times hostile divisions became intermingled in confusion; and, hand to hand, bayonet crossing bayonet, and sword clashing against sword, they fought with the ferocity of demons.

"I have often read of the horrors of war but here we saw it in reality; we could not hear any shouting of victory on anyside, but there was awful carnage and slaughter; and at sundown, the field, as it appeared, was crimson with blood. We all gazed at the grand spectacle till the sun had passed out of view in the golden west, when the phenomenon disappeared.

"The view was so magnificent and attractive that we never thought of taking notes at the time, so we can only give a very meagre account of this battle. I have never witnessed a battle raging before, but I will say this: I have followed the sea for well nigh thirty years, and of course when upon it am always at the mercy of the waves, but I greatly prefer the sea to having to stand in a battlefield.

"Next day we went ashore in Sydney and asked if any of the inhabitants had seen the sights that were visible in the clouds the day before. We were informed that no one had seen it."

Forerunners

No book of this type would be complete without at least one tale of a forerunner. There are so many to choose from it was difficult, but this particular tale was related by a fellow student in a folklore class, and had a ring of truth, and presence of modern times, I could not resist.

The story is one of a father and son. The son, an Island lad true, had joined the army during the great war and was later transfered to the navy. In that service he sailed on the ship, *Athabasca*.

One night the father heard his son come into the house, drop his kit bag on the floor, and sit down in a kitchen chair to remove his military boots, dropping the heavy footwear, one at a time, to the floor.

Then, his father heard the lad's footsteps on the stairs as he went up to bed.

I was an odd occurrence, for in his last missive home the son had told his father that he would be putting to sea, aboard the *Athabasca*. He should, his father knew, be aboard ship at that very time.

Upon investigating, he found no sign of his son, and returned to bed. We do not know what the father felt, whether he put the incident down to a dream, or sensed a terrible foreboding. The latter is suspected because, as it was related:

The father was quite good at feeling things — read tea leaves, "would make a good fist of it too."

If he read "feelings" correctly that night, it was to be with great mourning, for during the very same hours of darkness, the *Athabasca* was torpedoed and sent to the bottom of the sea, taking his beloved son to a watery grave.

The Phantom Train

A forerunner of a different kind was experienced many times in Island lore. This is one of the best known tales of such an event.

Picture a beautiful December day with brilliant sun causing the snow blanketing the landscape to sparkle like diamonds. Hardly the type of day for an apparition to appear! Yet in 1885 just such an occurrence happened in Wellington, a small village located west of Summerside, which at the time boasted a flour mill, saw mill, cloth mill, a couple of stores, a church, doctor, and post office.

A state of excitement prevailed at the mill house where final preparations for a wedding were under way. Nearby at the mill pond the young folk were skating. Mrs. John Coulson relates that they were using skates invented by the village blacksmith, "made with files inserted in blocks of wood, straps and buckles, and known as woodstocks."

Frivolity was forgotten when Dan, fifteen, of the mill house family, skated too close to where the water flowed into a flume to turn the wheels of the mill. The thin ice gave way and Dan was in the water. John, an older brother, rushed to the rescue but also went through the ice. It was only the action of a Mrs. Davis who was crossing the dam that prevented a double tragedy. She ventured onto the ice, and held John by the hair until he could be rescued.

Imagine the shock of a household preparing for a wedding, then suddenly plunged into a place of mourning.

Later that day at the witching hour of midnight, a train

was heard and its light beamed across the front of the house, lighting it in an astonishing manner, before the train roared to a nearby bridge where it stopped long enough for passengers to board. It was observed by some forty people as the usual engine with two passenger cars, bright lights spilling across the snow as the train continued on its way.

Not an unusual event, one would think, and yet the time was wrong — all scheduled trains had passed for the day. And even more mystery was to be revealed.

Among those at the mill house that night was a young lad who worked for the railroad as a section man, James Ferguson, of Summerside. He had arrived by way of a pumped trolley car for the purpose of courting one of the daughters of the house. Thinking that all the trains of the day had passed, he had left the trolley car on the track at the station.

When James heard the train whistle he, along with a couple of friends, ran to the station to remove the trolley car before the train crashed into it. They struggled the car off the track as the strong light bore down on them. And then, at the last minute, the train faded away into obscurity.

Those present were frightened indeed, wondering what the coming of this phantom train could foretell. At dawn, after huddling together all night, they checked with Summerside to see if the train had been real, but were told that no train had travelled those tracks that night.

No explanation for the appearance was ever given, but some suggested the ghost train came to take the soul of the unfortunate Dan directly to heaven.

The Phantom Bell Ringers: A Story of the Auld Kirk of St. James

J. Edward Rendle, in introducing this tale back in the beginning of the century, said that their era was one in which phenomena have attracted more attention than ever before. "Nearly all of us believe in a future state, but

how vague and ineffective this belief with the majority of persons; the number of people believing in Ghosts, a belief they allow to sit very lightly on their minds — they are afraid they will be called superstitious, a title convenient to attach to whatever we do not want to believe ourselves. But among these we find some who are not fearful of that bugbear, "Superstition," the gentleman who furnished the facts embodied in this peculiar incident being one of them. Many an ancestral home, and many a sequestered spot in wood or vale, have some tale of supernatural manifestation connected with them — a weird legend handed down from father to son, a record of a woman's crime or of a man's perfidy; but, as a rule, the visitant from the other world seeks retirement, and but seldom ventures into crowded streets, or public places. Some exceptions there are, of course, to this unwritten law, and among these we find the ghost, or " 'Ghosts of old St. James'."

My own theory is that the appearance of these "ghosts" was an incidence of a forerunner of death, bringing warning of a tragedy in the making.

St. James Church, the first Presbyterian place of worship in Charlottetown, is one of the oldest Protestant churches in the city, being opened for worship in 1828, and its walls have witnessed the triumphs and success of many celebrities of the town. The Rev. James McIntosh, the Rev. Robert M'Nair, the Rev. William Snodgrass, and the late lamented Rev. Thomas Duncan, and some others, have stood in its pulpit and received the ovations and attention of enraptured congregations. A strange place indeed for a ghost to select, but the fact of its appearance can be attested to by many. The story I am about to narrate is no fiction, and though names are altered, the occurrences referred to are all based upon facts that actually took place.

It was one of those sober and rather melancholy days in the early part of the autumn, when the shadows of the morn and evening almost mingle together; my friend Capt.

Cross, who had risen with the sun that morning, could be seen making his way into town from his home, a little way out on the Brighton road; my friend was early astir, hastening to the stables of the "Royal Oak," to look after a valuable horse that a few days before had arrived in town from his father's estate in Devon.

The Captain had almost reached Black Sam's Bridge when he heard, as he thought, a ship's bell ringing — it was quite clear and distinct to him — eight bells. The Captain was confounded, the sound did not appear to come from the sea; rather as it were from the heart of town. He stopped and heard the ominous sound again; this time he thought it was some vessel on her way out of the harbour, and the wind had carried the sound to him across the Pond.

He started on again, and hastened to make up the time he had lost by this strange occurrence. He had reached the corner of Pownal Street when he heard the bell again; no given number, but a continual dreary toll, as if it were some fog bell on some rock-bound coast. The Captain now thinking it was some foreign ship entering our harbour and, not knowing the channel, was nearing the shore, made his way to the small bridge at the entrance gates to Government House. Here he stopped and scanned the bay — he looked up and down, no vessels seemed astir, the *Fairy Queen* had not yet left for Pictou. There was a strong wind blowing. It swept in from the Straits, ruffling the surface of our placid harbour, and making it quite difficult for three Indians in a native canoe who were paddling their way from their encampment at Warren's Farm to the landing place at Pownal wharf. Here he again heard the bell, this time in the town again. He thought no church bell would ring at this early hour. What could it be?

The Captain now became deeply interested in his strange quest, forgetting all about his horse. He retraced his steps up Kent Street, and drawing near Pownal Street he heard the sound again, this time coming, he thought, from the belfry of the Kirk. Knowing it was unusual for the bell to ring at that still early hour, he decided to investigate the seeming mystery.

He crossed the street to Miss Macdonald's corner, walking up Pownal Street till he came to Fitzroy; here he heard the St. James's Church bell, no mistake, toll eight times, and lowering his eyes from the belfry to the entrance door, he there beheld on its very threshold three women dressed in some white material, with uncovered heads and feet. The women seemed not to notice him as he now made his way toward them. The bell now struck again, and on glancing up, he saw through the apertures the form, as he thought, of another woman; when he lowered his eyes it was but to see the church doors close upon the three that stood on the steps. As he reached the church door, Davy Nicholson, the Kirk sexton, turned the corner from the manse, where he (Davy) had been inquiring the cause of the bell-ringing at such an unseemly hour, and not receiving a satisfactory answer, decided to investigate for himself.

They both tried the church doors and found them securely fastened, and on looking through the small windows at the side of the door saw the retreating form of a woman ascending the steps that led to the belfry.

The sexton now made off to the manse for the key, leaving the "gallant" Captain on guard, who, above the roar and whistle of the wind, which was now blowing a gale, could hear the sound of foot-falls and voices in the tower above.

The sexton, accompanied by the minister of the Kirk at that time, Dr. Snodgrass, now arrived on the scene. The door being unlocked, the trio made their way up to the belfry. The wind twisted and twined itself about the giddy stairs, and made the very tower shake and shiver, as they ascended the ladder that led to the belfry, which was reached by a small trap-hatch, that had to be shut down when the bell was rung from above. The sound of the peal was heard again by the sexton and Capt. Cross who were climbing the ladder; Dr. Snodgrass, who was in the chamber beneath failed to hear it on account of the moaning and creaking of the tower at the time. Davy Nicholson was the first to throw up the hatch and gain access to the belfry, the Captain following close after. The hatch being closed to make room for the both to stand under the bell, they together examined the apartment, Davy putting his head out one of the small openings in the steeple where a view of the exterior of the belfry might be obtained. Inside and outside there was no one to be seen, though when they had reached the belfry the bell was still vibrating. Davy blamed the wind for the mystery, notwithstanding he having acknowledged to have seen the women going up the stairs from the first floor to the chamber above, but the Capt. still claimed that "there was a woman in it" somewhere.

Descending to the porch below, where the Doctor waited for them seeking to find out the cause of the unseemly disturbance, the Captain narrated to Dr. Snodgrass his peculiar adventure of the morning. The Doctor admitted that the bell might have rung, though he thought it was hardly possible; ridiculed the idea of either the Captain or sexton seeing the women. The sexton repudiated his statement about seeing the women ascend the stairs but the "power of the church," embodied in the minister, had no terror for the Captain, who still stoutly maintained that he had seen the women, and their appearance had left a lasting impression on his mind.

The church being locked up again, the minister and sexton returned home, the Captain proceeded to attend his horse, and the obscure events of the morning passed from their minds. Through the day the Doctor learned that the housekeeper at Dr. Mackieson's and several others in the vicinity of the Kirk had heard the bell at the same hour as the sexton and the Captain.

In the afternoon of the same day, Friday, October 7th, 1853, the sad intelligence that the mail steamer *Fairy Queen* had been lost in the strait between Pictou Island and Cariboo, and seven lives lost, four ladies and three men, three of whom were members of St. James's Church congregation, recalled to the minds of the parties interested the strange events of the morning, the appearance of the women, and the ringing of the bell, which was thought by Capt. Cross to have sounded like a ship's bell. To the above mystery I can offer no satisfactory solution. Life — for the present we are but half alive — is full of the marvellous. That we may understand more of the marvellous capacities latent in ourselves, and of the phenomena which surround us, is the object for which this narrative has been written.

J. Edward Rendle

Loss of the Fairy Queen

This accounting of the loss of the Fairy Queen *comes to us from* An Island Scrap Book *written, edited, and compiled by Benjamin Bremner and published in Charlottetown in 1932.*

The loss of the *Fairy Queen* is the story of a tragedy such as has been seldom recorded in the pages of Island history — a story of disaster, heroism, and base treachery. The dismal human trap, miscalled a steamboat, was, it appears, in a wretched condition as to hull and equipment, before making her trial trip across the Northumberland Straits, on her way to Charlottetown to take up the service between the latter port and Pictou, N.S. It seems that she underwent but a cursory inspection as to machinery, equipment, and safety devices, that she was newly painted to hide her rottenness and deformity, and that her crew was composed of a lot of coarse ruffians who did not hesitate to insult the passengers. This was bad enough, but when it is added, that her owners were previously warned of her very unsafe condition by competent judges, against starting on a sea trip, and that she was a condemned ship before leaving the Bay of Fundy, it should be sufficient reason for her detention in port. Notwithstanding all these warnings, her owners allowed her to proceed on her ill-fated journey. Before reaching the mainland, a violent storm came up, which an ordinary good vessel could have weathered, but the *Fairy Queen,* unable to stand the strain, went to pieces, causing the drowning of seven passengers — four women and three men. The other passengers, who managed to form a raft out of the cabin deck, managed to reach the shore in safety, after having exhausted all their energies endeavouring to save their fellows. Before this, the cowardly crew and captain stole the only boats, and left the passengers to their fate.

Mr. Lepage, in the first volume of the *Island Minstrel,* gives a vivid description of the disaster, and of the heroic efforts of the survivors to save their fellow-passengers, also of the dastardly conduct of the crew. I am here giving a small part of his verses on the terrible happenings.

> Sad is the burden of my song,
> A tale of death and human wrong,
> Involving deeds of such disgrace
> As seldom shame the human race.
> No fancy sketch! no trifling theme!
> Ah! would it were an airy dream!
> But sternest truth — which takes the form
> Of midnight murder in a storm!
>
> Seldom by mortals has been seen
> A boat like that same *Fairy Queen:*
> While all must hope, as honest men,
> Her like may not be seen again!
> By judges good pronounced a bore
> When first she voyag'd to our shore;
>
> Without proportion, ropes, or strength;
> And, from her most prodigious length,
> By superstition, judged to be
> The genuine "Serpent of the Sea!"
>
> Old, rotten, leaky, insecure;
> And, like a sepulchre, impure,

Where bones amid corruption lie,
Was paint-besmeared to please the eye

Her Crew! and who or what were they?
In sooth, 'tis very hard to say!
What were they? is it asked again?
No British seamen — that is plain.
Who ever heard of British tars
By frightful shipwreck or by wars
In peril placed — deserting there
The lives entrusted to their care?

So fares the brave! but Fate decrees,
On quiet land or stormy seas,
the coward's memory shall rot,
For infamy is best forgot.

Safe from the wreck and billows' roar
The Crew and Captain reach the shore.
Ashore and safe? no! still they fear,
For Lydiaard's threat rings in the ear,
"If Providence my life shall spare,
And such a trust e'en here I dare,
You'll rue your baseness by-and-by;
We'll meet again at Philippi?

For reasons which it will be apparent on reading this
mystery it seems appropriate that it should follow next after
the account of "The Loss of the *Fairy Queen*."

The Yankee Gale

The Great American Gales is not a legend, but one of our tales-true. Even today you can visit cemeteries all along the north shore of the Island and find the graves of sailors lost in one of the worst tempests of the sea to strike the waters of the Gulf. This accounting of the Gale was written by James D. Lawson and published in 1902. It gives insight into the magnitude of what happened, and the effect on just a few of the dozens of communities that felt the devastation. Statistics today show many more vessels lost, and I suspect more lives as well. I would assume that these numbers increased because the residents of 1851 would have no way of knowing of wrecks that went down off shore.

"For many years mackerel fishing has been carried on in the Gulf of St. Lawrence. On the north coast of Prince Edward Island is a wide stretch of the best fishing ground. A large number of vessels from the Atlantic coast of Nova Scotia and New England are engaged every summer in this fishery. Usually the weather is favourable, but old people still remember the great gale of 1851.

"The sun rose brightly on the morning of Friday, October 4th of that year. The sky was cloudless; the air balmy; the wind a gentle zephyr. The Gulf of St. Lawrence was "calm as innocence asleep." More than a hundred schooners with all their sails set — a magnificent sight — were standing in towards the Island which lies in "The Bay," as the American fishermen generally call the Gulf, in the form of a crescent, the captains of these schooners doubtless thinking that their prey was in the shallow water near the coast. Large catches were frequently made in those days late in the season, but few fish, if any, were caught that morning. As the day wore on the sky was of a grayish color and by evening was black and wild-looking as if it betokened an impending tempest. At about 4 o'clock the fleet stood off, the wind blowing freshly from the southeast.

"But too late, alas! The wind veered to the east, then to the north-east, and blew terrifically, rendering it impossible for most of the schooners to work clear of the land or to lie at anchor and outride the storm.

"After sunset a heavy swell arose on the Gulf. The sailors looked uneasy and the skippers watched their glasses with serious faces. Fortunately for many of the vessels the Island coast is not rock-bound, as it is for the most part on the Atlantic seaboard.

"The following morning — Saturday — how memorable because so awful. What wind! What rain! What devastation! The water was convulsive; the beach a seething mass of foam; the roar of the Gulf deafening and its appearance terrifying but truly majestic, and the sailors in a life and death struggle with the raging winds and waves. And as the day advanced the storm grew worse. Towards evening the wind shifted to the north. The night that followed was indescribable. At ten o'clock the storm reached its height and continued with undiminished fury until four o'clock the next morning, the rain all the while falling in torrents. Continuing all day Sunday it gradually subsided towards evening. During its continuance it was impossible to see much beyond the offing by reason of the heaviness of the rain and density of the spray; consequently the landsmen were largely ignorant of the ordeals that were taking place at sea.

"It is impossible to give anything like a detailed account or even to enumerate the many disasters that occurred, but a very few with their main features may suffice. Behind Cavendish, an agricultural district, situated about twenty-five miles to the north of Charlottetown, the capital of the Island, was a wreck in which could be seen the mutilated forms of thirteen men lashed to the rigging and almost naked owing to the rigour of the breakers. Nearby was a water-logged hull fast aground. When the vessel was boarded the crew — ten in number — were found dead in the cabin.

"In an adjoining cove still another vessel was aground, in which were fourteen men, none of whom had tasted food since the gale arose and it was then Sabbath morning. Starving and with no prospect of relief at hand, the men were desperate. As a last resort they made two empty casks fast to ropes and threw them into the water. Presently these came ashore and were secured by the landsmen. The ropes by the latter were quickly fastened to a tree growing on the bank and by that means four were safely rescued. Soon after that a tremendous wave lifted up the hull and landed it hard by the cliff. Fortunately all remaining on board sprang to the land and ran up the slippery bank.

"At Rustico, another farming settlement adjoining Cavendish at its eastern side, three schooners were wrecked within five miles of each other — The *Franklin Dexter*, of Dennis, Mass., U.S., manned by a crew of ten; the *Skipjack*, N.S., by a crew of twelve, and the *Mary Moulton*, Castine, by a crew of fourteen. The *Mary Moulton* was smashed to pieces. The unfortunate crew lie buried in Cavendish Cemetery. The *Skipjack* was beached dismasted with a hole in her side and a balance reef in her mainsail, the supposition being that she was "laying too," and was run down by another schooner. The remains of those on board were buried in the graveyard of the Episcopal Church, Rustico.

"The *Franklin Dexter* was owned by Capt. Wickson but sailed by Capt. Hall. Capt. Wickson's four sons and his nephew were on board. Three of the sailors forming the crew were found lashed to the rigging. Their bodies were horribly lacerated, their clothes being torn into shreds. The other members of the crew had disappeared. As soon as the aged parents of the Wickson boys heard of their sad fate, their mother prevailed upon their father — an old gentleman of seventy — to hasten from Dennis to the scene of the disaster and bring home, if possible, their bodies for interment in the family plot. When he arrived at Rustico, Capt. Wickson recognized some of his sons' clothes drying on a fence. As most of the bodies of the crew had been found and buried it was necessary to have them exhumed. On the lid of the first coffin being removed, Capt. Wickson fainted, and on being restored to consciousness he fainted again and again, and little wonder, for the lifeless form of his son was then exposed to view before him. He soon identified two more of his sons and his nephew. As he searched the shore day after day for the body of his remaining son he became very despondent, having been unsuccessful. His case elicited such universal sympathy that the inhabitants general joined him in the search. At length the body was recovered. The five coffins were put in a large packing case and placed on board the schooner *Seth Hall* which lay near, bound for Boston. Capt. Wickson proceeded to Charlottetown and took the steamer for the city. Reaching his home at Dennis, at the time expected, he met his relatives and friends, who mingled their tears with his as they listened to his touching story. But waiting and longing and hoping and praying for the arrival of the schooner with her precious freight brought her not, for the *Seth Hall* was lost at sea and never heard of more. The inhabitants of the port from which she sailed did not at all wonder at that, for, before weighing anchor, the Captain cursed the storm, and the devastation it made and impiously defied the God of the wind and weather to prevent him from reaching his destination.

"At the rear of Stanhope, another farming district, the writer's native place, fourteen miles from the capital, the schooner *Nettle*, of Truro, Mass., was stranded with four seamen washed overboard. Even yet some persons in this locality have distinct but melancholy recollections of the survivors weeping over their fallen comrades. And people there, now up in years, well remember the nervousness of women and children; especially after night, on account of the dead bodies on the shore.

"On Monday morning, between East Point and North Cape — the extreme points of the Island — in the long sweeping bay, a distance of more than one hundred and thirty miles, lay, it was estimated, eighty wrecks and about one hundred and sixty lifeless men.

"The following is taken from *Haszard Gazette*, then published in Charlottetown, dated Tuesday, November 10th, 1851:

"The Gale at Prince Edward Island"

"The Herald, Newbury Port, U.S., of Friday, contains the following authentic account of the late disaster at Prince Edward Island: —

"The committee who went down to Prince Edward Island, on behalf of the owners of fishing vessels belonging to this port, returned last night and brought accounts of all our vessels except two, from which nothing had been heard on Saturday last, when they left the Island.

"We have been furnished by Capt. Robert Barley and Capt. George Knight, with a complete list of the vessels lost on the Island. Of the vessels belonging to this port forty-four are safe and nineteen are lost, and two, the *Actor* and the *Augustus* not heard from.

"The masters of the schooners *Fulton Ruby*, *Montano* and *Griffon*, had chartered an English brig for $1,050 to bring up their fish.

"The committee estimate that although some vessels have undoubtedly been lost at sea with all their crews, the whole number of vessels ashore and lost will not exceed one hundred and fifty. The following is a list of the lives thus far known to be lost and the names of the vessels to which they belonged: —

VESSELS	MEN LOST
Statesman of Newburyport	10
Traveller, of Newburyport	8
Balema, or Portsmouth	10
Lion, of Castine	6
Franklin Dexter, of Dennis	10
Nettle, of Truro	4
Harriet Newell, of Harwich	2
Fair Play, of Portland	11
Flirt, of Gloucester	13
Mary Moulton, of Castine	12
Vulture, of Newburyport	1
Native America	2
America, of Lubec	9
	98

' "Several unknown vessels, it is supposed, foundered at sea. The committee visited the wreck of one of about eighty or ninety tons, a mile outside of Malpeque Harbor, but could not ascertain her name. She had an eight-square bowsprit, and from this they judged that she was either a Gloucester or Provincetown vessel. She appeared to have foundered at her anchors.

' "*The News*, Gloucester, Massachusetts, of October 29, says that the Lieut. Governor of Prince Edward Island, had issued a proclamation directing all officers of the Revenue, Magistrates and other subjects of Her Majesty to render all aid in their power to the unfortunate fishermen of the United States, who were wrecked on the northern coasts of that island and especially to exert themselves for the preservation of property and its restoration to the rightful owners; but it appears from what we learn of our fishermen who returned from the scene of the late disaster that this proclamation, though evincing the generous humanity of the

Lieutenant Governor of the Island, was unnecessary, for they all speak in the warmest terms of gratitude of the universal hospitality and kindness which they and all the ship-wrecked men received at the hands of those generous and humane islanders. In the midst of the storm they were on the beach to render every aid in their power to save life. After it had abated they cheerfully offered their services to assist in the preservation of property. They bore from the wrecks the bodies of those who had perished, prepared them for the grave at their own expense, and administered to them the last sad rites of humanity. Nor was that all; they opened their doors to those who had no shelter; fed and clothed the destitute, and bestowed upon the sufferers every possible assistance which could alleviate their misfortune, and every attention that humanity could devise. At the instance of many of our returned townsmen, our exchanges at Halifax and the P.E. Island papers are requested to make known to their readers the feelings of grateful remembrance in which the wrecked fishermen of Gloucester will always hold the generous hospitality extended to them in their misfortunes.' "

These ties between residents of the Island and New England have always been strong. A fact most often credited to the number of men who went to the woods of New England to earn high wages in the logging camps. Perhaps the bonds established during the days when U.S. fishermen plied the waters off the north shore, and particularly during the Yankee Gale, are equally to be credited for the link which remains strong to this day.

Crossing
at the Capes in Winter

Benjamin Bremner related just one of the fatalities which occurred during the ice-boat era, in An Island Scrap Book.

"To write up a thorough sketch of the old-time crossing between the Island and the mainland in winter, before the advent of the ice-breaking steamers, whose heroic and indefatigable commanders endeavoured, with but partial success, to overcome the barriers of the ice-bound Straits of Northumberland in the anxious days preceeding the car ferry service, is a rather difficult task for me.

"The earliest record of crossing the ice between the Island and the mainland, appears to date some time before 1827, when the mails were carried from Wood Islands to Pictou Island and thence to Pictou, a distance from P.E. Island about twenty-four miles. It took a long time and was a dangerous experience, so it frequently happened that weeks would elapse without a mail being received on either side.

"But it was the Cape Traverse and Cape Tormentine route that became the settled one for the winter mail and passenger service. In 1827 the pioneer trip was made on this route by Neil Campbell and Donald McInnis, the distance being about nine miles from shore to shore.

"Before the Federal Government assumed control of the ice boat service, the latter frequently proved to be a hazardous and even dangerous undertaking, sometimes attended with disaster and more than once with fatal results; the greatest calamity in its history resulting from a crossing attempted in March, 1855, when the parties concerned left the Tormentine shore in two boats, and had proceeded over one-half the required distance when they were caught in a severe snow-storm, accompanied by zero weather. After battling with the elements for over twenty-four hours, the boats' crews and passengers were forced to succumb and take shelter on the ice behind one of the upturned boats. The other boat was then broken up to make fuel to endeavor to keep the travellers from freezing to death. In the meantime their food had run out, and they had to kill a dog, which was eaten by the passengers and boats' crews to keep them from starvation. In this condition they continued until the third day out, when the drifting ice carried them almost back to the mainland shore, where the survivors were rescued by people of the locality, and taken care of, too late, alas! to save one of the passengers from death by exposure. The unfortunate victim was James Henry Haszard, third son of James Douglas Haszard, Esq., the Queen's Printer for P. E. Island. Mr. Haszard the younger, aged 18, was a medical student at Harvard University, and his tragic and early death cast a deep gloom over the people of his native City, on the receipt of the sad news. Most of the survivors were severely frost-bitten, one of whom had to submit to the amputation of parts of both feet. This was Richard Johnson, another medical student, and son of Dr. Henry A. Johnson of Charlottetown, both of whom were prominent physicians here some years past.

"Since that time there have been some severe happenings in ice-boat crossings — the worst of which took place in February, 1885, about a month before my first experience in this mode of travelling. There were several frost-bitten people in the February trip, the most unfortunate victim being a Mr. Glidden, connected with the firm of J. H. Myrick

& Co. of Tignish, P.E.I. Mr. Glidden had to suffer the amputation of fingers and toes on both hands and feet.

"Closely following the date of the disaster just mentioned, the Federal Government took over the control of the service, and in March of the same year I took my first trip on the "tramp and haul" journey with the strap across my shoulders.

"The boats used in the service were about eighteen feet in length, and in addition to the keel were shod with runners for their easier movement along the ice. When coming to open water, all hands would spring into the boats, which were rowed by the crews until again reaching ice pans, when all would step from the boats, each passenger and boatman passing a strap over one shoulder and under the opposite arm — the other end of the strap being attached to the boat in case of accident, and thus tramp alongside, hauling the boat until next coming to open water or to firm landing on the shore. Each boat was manned by five men — one of whom was the captain.

In this manner the unenviable trip was made. Sometimes, when the wind was favorable a sail would be hoisted, which would help considerably. The passengers, in addition to paying their fares, had the added privilege of helping to drag the boats across the ice. For a tyro, it was at first a trying experience, but after a while one got used to it, as was said "about the man that was hanged". I have made, I think, three round trips, and I do not long for further of the kind. This service was kept up even after the advent of ice-breaking steamers, when the latter were ice-bound, and occasionally even down to the dawn of the Car-Ferry service. So it will be seen that the Islanders were a long-suffering and very patient people regarding "continuous communication" with the mainland of Canada.

"Perhaps the most trying time to the patience of the travelling public was from January to March, 1905 — "The Big Winter", as it was called, when the winter steamers were tied up — one in Georgetown and the other in Pictou for over four weeks, but one trip having been made during that time (a god-send to the boat men of that year), when the snow fell almost continuously, until the drifts reached the telephone-wires in some places; when all trains were blocked for nearly two months, and the mails had to be carried by relays of horses and sleighs to all parts of the Province. This winter had its compensations, however, for many parties resulted from the tie-up, especially in hotels, which were crowded with travellers, functions in which the townspeople participated, thus contributing to make a very happy time which otherwise might not have materialized."

Horse Through the Ice!

Horses were commonly taken out onto the ice until quite recently. Primarily they were there for two reasons: to dig mussel mud or to travel a shorter route between centres. Most of the time this worked well. Winds usually blew the snow off the ice so that travel was much easier, and the distance to town or a call greatly shortened. Thaw, however, was a culprit which never failed to invade the ice, weakening it, cracking it, until it was not safe to be on. Unfortunately, heavy snows did not always melt on land fast enough causing people to stretch the season for "just one more trip" on the ice.

Thus, horse through the ice was not an uncommon happening; however, like all things a pioneer faces, this was not an insurmountable catastrophe, but rather a problem to be coped with. The following two incidents are among dozens I have heard of where a horse was choked to save its life.

One Dougald McKinnon, resident of Mt. Buchanan in the 1860s, was crossing the ice to Charlottetown from Gallows Point (Earnscliffe), when his horse broke through and began to flounder in the freezing water.

First efforts convinced Dougald that he could not get the

horse out on his own, so his teen-aged daughter Margaret, who was travelling with him, was dispatched for shore.

Her solitary journey over the ice was cut short, however, for a crowd of men had seen the accident and rushed out from Gallows Point to lend their assistance. These fellows were well experienced with such happenings, and came equipped with the paraphernalia needed to haul Dobbin (or whatever the poor languishing creature was called) from the icy bay. Not far behind was a man with a team of horses.

By the time the driver arrived an argument was heating up about just how to go about getting the animal back up on its feet — planted on a solid underfooting. Some said choke it so that it would float without too much plunging about.

Dougald nayed that idea, fearing the ruination of the animal. He was overruled by the driver who it is said, announced, "We will hang the horse and let Dougald go damn."

Quicker than a wink the deed was being done, and the horse popped onto solid ice — unfortunately appearing to be rather dead. Driver wasted not a word; he dragged the carcass across the ice, and right up to his homestead where he caused the horse to be dragged right into the house. Dougald had followed this procession, raging and ranting about his loss.

One can only imagine his tongue being silenced as he saw the animal placed as close to the warmth of the fire as it is possible to get the carcass of a horse, and even more incredible, a potion of the cherished family rum poured down its throat. The family blankets were taken from their very beds and every man present took a turn rubbing and kneading the animal back to life.

Strange to say, this treatment was soon effective, and ere long "Dobbin" was on his feet and ready for many more years of life.

The ranting Dougald quickly became a humble man when he saw his beloved animal back on its feet, and he developed a loyalty to the Driver which was to last to the end of his life.

In the days before commercial fertilizers, mud from rivers and bays was hauled up from under the water by using horses out on the ice to dredge the bottom. This mud, rich in lime from shells of shellfish and decaying matter from the sea, was generally termed "mussel mud."

Many tales are still heard today of happenings out on the ice. Most prevalent are those concerning the great danger, to both man and his horse, of falling through the ice. David Weale recounted one such tale in an article which appeared in *The Island Magazine* in 1978:

"Occasionally a horse, or even a team would fall into the hole, causing great excitement and commotion. There was a special technique for saving such animals which was practical in all parts of the Island. The struggling horse, it was discovered, could be more easily rescued if he were first choked. According to Lorne Wiggington:

" 'When a horse would get in you'd hear the shout and everybody would come running. They'd put a noose around his neck and some would catch hold of his tail, and some would put a rope on the girth that went around him, and everybody would get a hold of something to pull. When everybody was ready — this rope around his neck — they gave it a jerk and tightened it, and then when the horse started to choke and he bounced up, and as he bounced out of the water everybody pulled and they landed him right over the side. Oh, slick — just like a balloon.' "

"The shivering animal would then be rubbed down vigorously, usually with some hay from the sleighs and, in most cases, would be none the worse for the experience."

Occasionally, the heat from the mussel bed would prevent ice forming, thick enough to hold man and beast and their equipment. Enterprising souls would then cut off great pans of ice, and float into a good position for the digging. When the load began to sink the ice, they would float it to a handy place for transferring the smelly 'black gold'."

Dead Man's Pond

There are many versions of how this pond, located in the woods of Charlottetown's Victoria Park, got its lurid name. My favourite is the Micmac spirit, coming to claim intruders.

It is said that Dead Man's Pond is the gateway to the residing place of a great, but vengeful, Indian spirit. On occasion, the spirit would take offense at those who invaded the solitude of his pond. Rising up from the deep, he would grasp all who swam in the water or even wandered close to the shore. Pulling them down to where the denizens of the deep lurked in waiting, he would steal their very souls, before spewing the body back up to act as a warning to others to stay far from the shores of the pond.

Another version of the naming of the pond is perhaps a little more believable to readers. In the early days of white settlement on the Island, the Governor threw a gala New Year's Eve ball. A woodcutter, a poor, but honest and trustworthy man, loaded his sleigh with the best burning wood and drove it to the Governor's residence to ensure warmth for the revellers. The Governor, grateful for the thoughtfulness of the woodcutter, gave him an extra stipend of gold in reward. It is thought that he was murdered and robbed for this gold and his body thrown in Dead Man's Pond.

Treasure was the culprit in our third version. Seekers had determined that pirates put into shore just at the point of land that is Victoria Park, and buried their booty in the woods. Years later the site was found, and treasure hunters began to dig a huge hole in hopes of finding the chests of gold. When they got down so deep the sky was just a pinprick above them, the side of their hole suddenly burst and water poured in from the Gulf. Storytellers, of course, state that this was the curse of the pirates working to protect the treasure. Some versions of this tale say that there is a tunnel, now filled with water of course, which gives access to Charlottetown Harbour. This tunnel acts as a protection against invaders in a similar manner to that theorized about on Oak Island in Nova Scotia.

There are other versions of the naming of Dead Man's Pond, almost as many as there are people's imaginations. These are my favourites. The pond is still said to be bottomless and a very dangerous place to be. It is fenced off now, but still easily found in the woods of Victoria Park.

Treacherous Travel

Travel was perilous indeed in the days before the automobile became the accepted mode for getting from one place to another. Winter was the most dangerous time. Freezing temperatures, snow, and ice made travel a great risk.

Anyone living away from a settlement or town limited their travel to one or two visits during the winter, and then only if absolutely necessary. For venturing away from the security of home or community could be dangerous, so dangerous that the cost was, all too often, life itself.

One of the things that would necessitate a journey in winter was the need for supplies. Albert King of Georgetown was born in 1900. He recalled one of those times when need overcame caution. It was the winter of 1917.

"The ice was so thick a man could walk from Georgetown to Souris, or keep on going to East Point if he wanted. Three boats made it through from Pictou to Panmure. The wife's father was a sailor then, on board the *Earl Grey*, oh, she was a beauty, that ship. Then there were the *Minto* and the *Stanley*. But, the *Earl Grey*, she was the lovely one.

We went out with horse and sleigh from Georgetown, over the ice to where the boats were lying off Panmure. We unloaded them through the portholes, mostly fruit and vegetables it was. And we loaded pork and black oats on board. What is black oats? That's a small hard oat, real good for horses.

We worked for three days and three nights without stopping, as soon as one boat was finished, we did the next. I was so tired I fell asleep holding onto the sleigh. I was 17 then and strong, but we worked. My God we worked."

This interview with Mr. King was done a few years ago when I worked at the local newspaper. He had also ridden the trains as a shoveller. They would sit upon the tender, and when they came to a drift would jump off and start to dig out. He remembered they used to get breakfast when working on the trains, potatoes and salt herring.

Mrs. John England of Loyalist Road related some less happy tales of travelling by horse and sleigh. The first incident occurred on the way back from Charlottetown.

"There were people, named Paposie, a French family, who went to town in a horse and sleigh. It came up cold — an awful night. They froze to death, sitting up in the sleigh.

They had left one or two children at home, and they both froze to death (she didn't mean the children but rather their parents). They had taken a little dog with them. There was a bad storm and it took two or three days for the horse to get home. When the children went out, they found the parents dead, but when they lifted the buffalo robe, the little dog was alive.

Hurrys bought the Paposie place (located on what is now known as the Hurry Road). They named the farm and their line of cattle after them. Jim Hurry used to tell that story".

Her second story involving horse and sleigh was a happier one. It concerned an old fellow who was going to Summerside, on the ice, driving a wood sleigh.

"The sleigh upset and him under it. The horse broke loose and was gone, and it rolled the sleigh over. When the horse got home, the relations went looking for him, and when they found him, he was still trapped under the sleigh mumbling, 'Never again, never again.'

They thought he meant never again would he use the horse, but it was really never again would he go anywhere without a screwdriver. He had a bottle of liquor, but nothing to open it with."

There are hundreds of tales of horses, sleighs, and the difficulty of winter travel, some of them adventures that were lived by people able to relate them even today.

Slightly Siberian Souris

This report gives a humorous look at travel at its worst in December, 1943. On the 28th day of the month, enlisted men from R.A.F. Base Charlottetown set off at 14.15 hours to pick up a sick airman from "The Novorisisk or Holmangrad or somewhere way out on the western front." We Islanders would recognize the area as East Baltic. The day they left on their fated trip was described as thus, "the sun was shining warmly on the rather dirty snow,"; in other words, it was nothing like the appalling winter conditions that are often coped with, even today.

"All went fairly well until we reached a point five miles beyond two farmhouses and a coca-cola stand, we believe to be known as Mount Stewart. At this juncture the ambulance had evidently had it — it lazily did an old time waltz, threw us all about, and came to rest on its side in the ditch.

We clambered out — the sun had gone down, and so had our spirits — not even a jeep in sight. One farmhouse evidently hadn't seen humans or the R.A.F. before — we got no advice and no telephone.

"Muffled up in the blankets we had brought for the patient, we trudged back up the hill to a smithy's place where we saw a Mark I sleigh. Here we succeeded in getting a lift for the four miles walk back to Mount Stewart. We lay on the soap-box floor, and though we closed our eyes, the horse made its presence felt in the ice chips of P.E.I. soil (something new added, not apple honey) which assailed our mouths and nostrils. It was confoundedly cold by the time we crawled out at the garage. So this was the lovely island we'd been posted to!

"After telephoning the Station Adjutant (whose chief worry was 'Oh God, this will mean at least six summaries of evidence on oath of course and maybe a court martial'), we attempted to restart the circulation of blood. When the blood reached our numb brains again, we perceived a train in the local C.N.R. station *believed* to be Tuesday's train en route for Souris (and the locality where we were bound for). Eventually we got in the train after buying a ticket, as we thought in a frightful hurry — but actually we could have spent another fifty minutes on the job before the train got under way.

Whether the train took in Summerside or not, we're not prepared to say, but eventually the *same evening* we arrived at a delightful coastal resort, by the name Souris (by the sea?). There was the usual Canadian station scene — though the station-master looked a bit puzzled at seeing the train, we believe. We made our way over various masses of frozen snow, rowing boats, and other indeterminate parapher-nalia, to the office of the R.C.M.P. It was a change to reach an atmosphere eighty degrees F. higher than the one we had just been existing through, and the high spot was managing to hear Don Messer and his Islanders just coming over the radio.

Here we were thankfully refreshed and fitted out with a coat, buffalo, R.C.M.P. type, ordinary, and cap to match. The corporal was, we thought, much too cheery about "the worst yet to come." He needn't have been so cheerful. We got into the police car and set off — we're prepared to swear — over a route hitherto untrodden by man or beast.

Four times we got out and pushed that beautiful Buick (with its eight cylinders) through an icy impasse, and on the two occasions we failed, we still had to push the four horses that were called in to help. The night was pitch-black, and the creak of chains and the glint of pairs of eyes high up were the only signs of life on the steppe (it must have been a steppe).

Finally the R.C.M.P. corporal said "this is the rendezvous — here the farmer will meet you with his sleigh and the journey into the unknown starts." We thought of the (?) beautiful meal we were missing in the Mess. Somewhere Bing Crosby would be dreaming of a White Christmas. We could hardly reach our cigarettes through the coats we had on, and our B.O. (Buffalo Odour) was becoming a trifle noticeable.

The car stopped, and choosing to die of exposure rather than of carbon monoxide poisoning, we turned off the engine and waited. Half an hour later the jingle of bells notified the approach of the final means of transport. We shook hands with the R.C.M.P. corporal, and resolutely and resignedly stepped into the Mark V type of sleigh. We could not see our pilot (or what do sleighs have?), but muffled words like "hang on here" reached us from time to time. We appeared to have to traverse first a hill resembling the "big dipper" at Blackpool, then we went across a lake and generally bounced over the uneven ground one skid low. We hung on with everything we'd got. Jingle bells, jingle bells. We thought of the awful annual job Santa Claus had, and guess he'd be prepared at times to exchange his vehicle for a tank at Bardia, or something. The stars had now come out, and illuminated a wild, uninhabited sort of scene — we turned now West, now North — the sleigh journey of approximately 45 minutes seemed like nights, and we wondered whether we'd ever reach East Baltic. Finally, the most welcome light we'd ever seen appeared, apparently from out of nowhere and we arrived — the horse evidently jumping for joy, nearly throwing us out of the sleigh — at the farm-house at last.

They lifted us out, and thawed us out over the kitchen range. We saw our patient, and prepared to spend our night with farmhouse fare, and folk lore. We left at the unearthly hour of five next morning, saying goodbye and promising to return — if we lived — in the Spring. Another type of sleigh was now used to accommodate the patient, and we lay on the straw looking up at the unconcerned stars, and the silent, black, fir trees, lining the route to Elmira (or some such Spanish frontier town). The coal furnace blazed light fitfully on six other unfortunates in the station waiting room, and, half an hour late, the nightly C.N.R. milk train roared in. All aboard and we were homeward bound, for Charlottetown and civilization again.

This tale of retrieving a downed airman had a happy ending, as did the following rescue which resulted in an Island lad being granted true hero status.

Fly Boys' Hero

Jack Meredith recalled the incident in a special Remembrance Day Programme done by Cathy Large of CBC in 1981. Mr. Meredith was on the R.A.F. Training Staff for three years, a wireless operator on one of the AVRO Ansons used by student navigators at the base.

"One of the biggest nuisances I found on the job was the student navigators being inexperienced. There is a tremendous difference between true north and magnetic north here on P.E.I. I think it's around 25 degrees. If the navigator added the 25 instead of subtracting it you didn't have to fly too long before you were way off. And it was always a case of using the radio ranges that were set up around the Maritimes. We would always find our way back — or at least I did anyhow." Jack Meredith.

Others, less experienced, did not always make it back to the base. It is not certain whether the plane in the following account got lost and ran out of fuel, or had an engine failure. It was known it did not return when expected.

The hero of this tale was one Carl Burke who, as a boy in Charlottetown, dreamt of becoming a pilot. Flying lessons were expensive in the depression of the 1930s, costing $10 an hour at the nearest flying school in St. John, New Brunswick. Burke was a determined young lad and managed to save enough from his $12 a week salary to get a license; then he saved enough to buy a small second-hand plane, and began flying passengers to the mainland for $50 a trip.

During the war, Burke became a trans-Atlantic ferry pilot, flying aricraft made in Canada to Great Britain where they were used to fight the Germans. During this period he and a fellow ferry pilot, Joseph Anderson, decided to start an airline in Atlantic Canada, which eventually became Maritime Central Airways and served the region for many, many years. Unfortunately, Mr. Anderson never saw the dream become reality, as he crashed and was killed on his final trip for the overseas ferry service.

In 1943, Carl Burke answered a call to rescue four fliers whose aeroplane had been forced down on a patch of drifting ice in the Gulf of St. Lawrence. They signalled for aid with their radio, but the planes sent out were too large to make a landing. There were none small enough on the Island.

Jack Meredith recalls the incident: "The aeroplane was part of a regular exercise, normally there was 12 planes went out on a navigational exercise for student navigators, and on the return trip this aeroplane went down on the ice. Whether it ran out of fuel or engine failure I don't know.

But radio messages went out from the downed plane. The operator on that aeroplane sent out messages and others that were on the exercise picked them up and were able to find them."

The R.A.F. planes circled their downed companions; unable to land, they waited for Carl Burke, praying the ice would hold together until he arrived. It must have seemed an interminable wait.

In response to the call for help Burke had to fly to Moncton to get a small two-seater plane that could be equipped with skies. He landed four times on the dangerous ice, taking one airman ashore each time.

"We circled until Captain Burke came with his little one (plane) but when he came it was time for us to get out because we were getting short of fuel," recalls Jack Meredith. "The ice broke up and the Anson went down. It was that close for those boys."

For this dangerous rescue Carl Burke was made an officer of the Order of the British Empire by King George VI.

Tea Hill Disaster

Our last tale associated with the "Boys in Blue" of the Second World War has a sad ending, and perhaps brings home the realities of just why the air bases were located on Prince Edward Island to train aircraft personnel. Death and war are painfully linked in all of our minds. Although these deaths were not caused by an act of war, it was war that caused the men to be in the situation that led to their demise. The following accounting is taken from the newspaper report of January 12th, 1942. Speculation that this disaster was made even more terrible by the fact that one pilot, failing an attempted rescue of a second plane which was damaged, killed his own crew, has made this an often-told tale of the past.

"Seven men were killed yesterday afternoon when two Royal Air Force planes from the Charlottetown airport crashed at Southport, about three miles from Charlottetown.

"Group Captain E.A. Blake, Officer Commanding at the

airport, announced the names of the men would not be released until their next of kin were notified.

"He issued the following statement last night:

"'Two Anson aircraft belonging to the Royal Air Force station Charlottetown, collided over Southport about three miles southeast of Charlottetown at about 3 p.m. on Monday, the 12th of January. Both aircraft crashed to the ground and one exploded on contact. The seven members of the crew of the aircraft were all killed, all but one being Royal Air Force personnel from the United Kingdom. The two aircraft struck the ground near Mr. H. J. Kennedy's farm near Tea Hill.'

"A number of persons saw the planes circling and diving over Southport and the Charlottetown Harbour area before the crash. A few said they actually saw the two planes collide. A wing appeared to be torn from one.

"Several held the belief the other plane attempted to get under the damaged machine and support it before it crashed.

"Three men were in one plane and four in the other. All were killed instantly.

"There was no fire after the crash.

"One plane was comparatively intact, but the other was smashed to splinters. One woman resident of Southport said she heard what sounded like an explosion after the planes struck the earth."

Speculators believed this noise was the damaged plane crushing the one beneath it. Jack Meredith remembered the day of the accident.

"The memory I had of that crash is watching the aeroplanes in the air. This particular day I wasn't flying, was watching these two aeroplanes in the air along with another chap at the airport. We saw them flying and fall.

"The fire department, rescue department had to send out their equipment from the airport. In order to get out of the main gate you had to pass where myself and this other chap were. And when we saw the wagon coming along we ran to jump on the side of it to go out to the scene.

"Whilst we were running it suddenly came to me, 'What am I doing this for — tomorrow someone may be running to see me.' So I just stopped and turned around and went back to the hanger. I knew the boys. I knew the boys that were in the aeroplane. The two pilots, one in each aeroplane, I flew with those two. I have their names in my log. So I didn't want to go.

"I just wasn't interested in seeing what was left."

Phantom Submarine Among the Evidence of a War that Came Too Close

The phantom ship was not the only mystery vessel to ply the waters around the Island. While I was inquiring about the phantom ship, it was suggested that I should look to other phantoms, such as the submarine that came and went in the Gulf of St. Lawrence, during the Second World War.

In all matters relating to the sea, Lorne Johnston from Montague is my "expert." He once wrote a column ("The Ole Salt" in the *Guardian* a couple of years or more ago) on the phantom sub, and we talked about its presence in the waters off the Island.

Lorne remembered talking with an officer from a *Fairmile*, a sub-chaser that acted as an escort for convoys of freighters that travelled up the Gulf during the war. These convoys went from Sydney, Cape Breton, to East Point, North Cape, Gaspé and on up the St. Lawrence to Montreal, presumably to stay close to shore and less exposed to the German submarines.

This fellow told of submarines being sighted off the bow, chase being given, and then the sub simply disappearing. It happened several times in several locations but, as Lorne says, one disappearance followed another through the summer of 1946 or 1947.

"Reports became so weird that many were never reported,' he said.

Fishermen were said to have sighted the sub about ten miles off shore all along the north shore and up towards Cape Bear. The Mounties even went to East Point and asked the fishermen to let them know when they saw the sub.

Lorne said that the man on the *Fairmile* claimed the sub was never destroyed, and that although the hiding place was never found, it was felt that it was a huge hole in the floor of the Gulf. This hole, or canyon, in the gulf floor is eight miles long, has an average width of two miles, and is seven to nine hundred feet deep. The hole can be seen on charts between the Magdalene islands and P.E.I.

At least one ship, *City of Charlottetown*, a corvette, was torpedoed in the Gulf, according to fishermen in East Point who were told about it by a Mountie.

There are some documented reports of fishermen who later realized that they had actually been doing trade with crewmen from the sub. Boats would meet out in the water, far from knowing eyes, and an exchange for cigarettes, fresh food, and such would take place. It is likely that these traders never knew the implications that could have been inferred from their trading with the enemy. Today they do, for it is difficult to find anyone with personal knowledge of such events.

This story, along with that of the German airship spotted over P.E.I., the German prisoners of war who were held on the Island, and the intensive training that was given to airforce personnel from Britain, the U.S., and Canada here on the Island, brings home just how close the war really was to residents of the Island.

I used to believe that Canadians were isolated from the realities of the war, but that was just not so in this province which has the highest per capita enlistment in the country. Those left at home felt the war almost as personally as those who went away.

Imagine the feeling of your men folk being gone, not

knowing how they were faring, and wondering if those with you were safe from the Germans whose presence was so near.

Of course, the people left at home must have felt more secure with "The Boys In Blue" buzzing overhead.

Great
Humming Bird of the Sky

*One of the best sources of information about the lives of
the boys in blue, who were stationed on the Island during
the Second World War, can be found in issues of* THE
GRAF, *the magazine of R.A.F., Charlottetown, P.E.I.,
which was published on the base.*

*These books are not easy to find these days, but a couple
of copies do exist at the P.E.I. Archives, and readers of
articles I have written on the topic have led others to kindly
loan me their treasured copies.*

*The following tale of a great humming bird from the sky
is taken verbatim from the April, 1943 issue of* THE GRAF.

"One cold grey morning, not so long ago, the drums of
the bush telegraph of the Magdalen Islands thumped
out the news ... 'Flash ... Flash... ' beat the drums,
'attention everybody ... One of the great Humming Birds of
the Sky has been injured and is lying at this moment a few
miles out on the ice; it has been there some hours now and has
not moved ... it is probably dead ... there is no danger.'

"The drums at the hands of a minor Walter Winchell spelt
out the news and the men of the Magdalens shook with
excitement that one of the Great Humming Birds of the Sky,
which they had often watched winging over their domain,
should be lying dead so near their shores.

"But more staggering news was in store for them; later that day the drums told how two White Lords of the Heavens had struggled across the ice from the Great Humming Bird of the Sky, clad in strange garments and tight fitting leather hats of which good earthly men knew nothing.

"The Head supernatural being was immediately dubbed 'He of the Sandy Upper-lip' and his disciple 'Big White Chief Dot-an-Dash' and were greeted with appropriate ceremony by the Island Chief, Black Horse, leader of the Dabatt tribe.

"They condescended to accept the food and drink, of the simple folk of the Magdalens, but each morning forced themselves away to visit the Great Humming Bird of the Sky whose dead carcass was slowly sinking in the ice. Black Horse told his people that they went to pray for the prosperity of the islands and a few days later it was clear that their prayers were being answered, for, from the heavens above came another Great Humming Bird of the Sky to drop gifts in white clouds on the Island. Black Horse brought the presents to He of the Sandy Upper Lip who was much relieved to find amongst them a small tin marked Bile Beans, containing tablets which He of the Sandy Upper Lip told Black Horse were all powerful and able to shift heaven and earth. Black Horse was duly impressed by the tablets and their effect on He of the Sandy Upper Lip.

"Then came the great day when another Great Humming Bird of the Sky alighted on the ice and blessed the Island with three more of its Sons, namely, the Mighty Lord Tech-Tech, the Little Lord Tech-Tech, and the Lesser Lord Tech-Tech, also named Irk. They joined their fellow gods and much was the rejoicing and planning. Every day they undertook their pilgrimage to the Great Humming Bird of the Sky armed with shovels and spanners and various other implements of prayer. To the people of the Magdalens they explained that they had been sent down to earth to resurrect the dead bird and loud was the jubilation when the

Great Humming Bird of the Sky breathed fire and sang again.

"Our story is almost over, for, that very day the Angels of the Tech-Tech Realm left in one of the Great Humming Birds of the Sky and on the following morning He of the Sandy Upper Lip and Big White Chief Dot-an-Dash were swallowed by the now fully recuperated Great Humming Bird of the Sky, which singing merrily all the while and with a final cry of delight, sped along the ice, lifted itself and flew. As Black Horse and his people watched from a respectful distance the Great Humming Bird of the Sky circled over them twice and then zoomed into the cold blue sky.

"And still Black Horse and his people watched until the bird was no more than a speck above the horizon, sorry that they were losing their new-found friends but happy that their hospitality would live in memory."

"Bye Now"

A gallant young airman lay dying,
At the close of a bright summer's day.
His comrades had gathered around him,
To carry his fragments away.

The aeroplane was piled on his wishbone,
The Vickers was wrapped round his head,
He wore a spark plug in each elbow,
'Twas plain he would shortly be dead.

He spat out a valve and a gasket,
As he stirred in the sump where he lay,
And then to his wondering comrades,
These brave parting words did he say.

"Take the manifold out of my larynx,
And the butterfly valve off my neck,
Remove from the kidneys the camrods,
There's a lot of good parts in this wreck.

"Take the piston rings out of my stomach,
And the cylinders out of my brain,
Extract from my liver my crankshaft,
And assemble the engine again.

"Pull the longeron out of my backbone,
The turn-buckle out of my ear,
From the small of my back take the rudder,
There's all of your aeroplane here.

"I'll be riding a cloud in the morning,
With no engine before me to cuss,
Take the lead from your feet and get busy,
There's another lad needing the bus."

They Made 'Em Tough

To understand the hardship and perseverance of the Islander to blessed well do just what he set out to do that day, one just has to look at the days of early train travel. Albert King of Georgetown still recalls the days when men dug out the tracks for the trains; for some it was just so they could get where they were going; for the unemployed it was mandatory to put food on the table. This is his accounting of just one storm, the like of which was duplicated time and time again, from one end of the isle to the other.

The winter of 1926 was a year for snow. "It was so high it covered the telephone poles and come right up to the upstairs windows of the houses," related Albert.

"Fourteen of us left Georgetown for Charlottetown with the train, drifts covering the tracks all along. We would sit up on the tender (that's the coal-car) and when we come to a drift, off we would hop and start shovelling. At Roseneath the snow was so high, 100 men come to dig out, three rows of men shovelling.

"At Charlottetown a train was sent to help with three engines. She backed up and run so damn hard at the snowdrift, the tracks just ripped up and the engines flew off into the snow. Took up to two days to heave those engines back on the tracks.

"We had a cook on board and one breakfast I remember real well, potatoes and salt herring it was. My it was good that.

"On the way back we run out of coal at Brudenell and we had to go up into the woods and cut down some hardwood to raise the steam to get home. Seventeen days it was before we got home."

Just to give you an insight into the type of Islander Albert recollected, let me tell you that in 1979, when he was out hauling lobster alone in the boat, his arm was caught under the keel in the hauler. "I had to climb overboard to get my arm loose and then climb back into the boat, it was a hanging just by a bit of skin, nearly off at the wrist. And I was bleeding like a devil too." Although another fisherman came to Albert's aid, he started the boat engine himself, travelled the six miles back to Georgetown and, after his daughter had driven him to hospital in Montague, another distance, walked himself into the operating room. His arm needed a steel brace in it and they replenished four bottles of blood, but "they fixed it as good as new."

Nigger – the Dog
That Would Not Die

Many strange tales involved animals, but more often as an adversary than as a friend. The story of Nigger comes from the Charlottetown air base of the British Royal Air Force established during the Second World War for the purpose of training airmen.

Nigger, a black retriever, was said to have won the right to "some recognition in the Camp" through his determination to live and be part of a life he obviously loved — as a member of the group of men learning to defend their country.

In 1942 an order went around the camp that all unregistered dogs must be destroyed.

Nigger, along with many miscellaneous pets, was collected by those assigned the dastardly mission, and taken away for destruction. The R.C.M.P. guaranteed that he was shot, but must have forgotten to tell Nigger, for he reported for duty the next day.

A second time Nigger was taken away, and once more he was "shot," and once more he reported back to camp.

Not to be outdone, the authorities took most drastic measures. The third time Nigger was sent away it was with an escort of police, and the Commanding Officer himself personally heard the shot which the Mounties guaranteed killed Nigger.

The period of mourning the coal black dog was short-lived. The very next day Nigger reported personally to the Commanding Officer's office.

Now, it is well-known that the British are a bit soppy about pets to begin with. Add to this the well-known tenet that after a man's hanging has failed three times he gets away with it, and you have just cause for Nigger being permanently reprieved.

The dog became a "most law-abiding citizen" and was reported to book out of camp each night and go to the Canadian Legion with the boys. He would return promptly on the last bus, report to the guardroom, and stay somewhere in camp. To his credit, the intelligent dog with a love of life was said never to have gone near the aircraft, never to have gotten into mischief, and to have been friendly to everyone.

Another dog that is fondly remembered by the men of the R.A.F. comes to us only by the name Big Red Dog. It will perhaps take a member of the armed forces to appreciate the joy that the animal brought to those who had adopted him as a mascot, because of their appreciation and understanding of rank.

Big Red Dog was born in Charlottetown, and when a well-grown puppy, insisted on boarding the postal wagon and living in the camp. He was deported several times, but was finally adopted by "A" Flight.

This dog became by way of a mascot in the camp. He was continually making trouble by not being chained up when he should be and by appearing in places where he should not. His chief dislike was civilians, especially in barrack blocks.

Big Red Dog was, however, said to be very democratic, and would make friends with "any AC.2." His degree of friendship varied inversely with the rank of the person he met. He would wag his tail to officers and even tolerate the Group Captain, but was known to attack an A.O.C.

The Bulldog
and the Bear

There are many, many tales of bears attacking people and animals, and of people retaliating against Mr. Bruin. So dangerous were these animals perceived to be that they were relentlessly hunted until gone. The gentleman who related this particular tale to one Joseph F. Doyle was an old man at the turn of the century, placing the time of the incident in the early 1800s. This is the old man's story.

"When I was a boy of fourteen my father sent me to work with a farmer in Lot 48. His farm fronted the East River, and, in the fall of the first year I was with him, I hauled a great deal of seaweed from the shore. This farmer had a vicious bull-dog, much dreaded in the neighbourhood. One evening he and I, each with a horse and cart, went for loads to the shore and the dog came with us. A pretty heavy wood skirted the river not very distant from where we got the seaweed, and our attention was soon drawn in that direction by the fierce barking of the dog, and the horrid growl of a big black bear which had come out of the wood on to the shore, where he and the dog stood at some little distance apart each apparently watching the chance of making an attack.

"We soon saw that the bear was not on the aggressive, but would turn and run away, only for a short distance at a time, as the dog would spring towards him immediately and try to catch him by the hind legs. Failure on the part of the bear either to strike his enemy or run away caused him to take to swim across the river. He had swum quite a little distance before the dog had decided to follow, but the latter swimming at a more rapid rate was overtaking bruin. When the bear saw that his chance of escaping the dog in this way was in vain, he stopped, and stood erect in the water awaiting the approach of the dog which came up furiously toward him. As soon as he came within reach the bear struck at him with both paws and in the same moment the dog had pinned him by the throat. A struggle followed for an instant, when both sank, and for some little time disappeared. When they arose to the surface they seemed to hold the same grips but the dog alone showed any signs of continuing the fight. There was a small boat on the shore, which the farmer used when needed to cross the river. This we launched and went out to the struggling beasts. As we neared them we noticed that the bear was lifeless and the dog still clinging to the hold he first got. We managed to get a line fastened to the bear and towed both ashore. Even then the dog held on, but we soon discovered that he could not extricate himself, as the claws of the bear had been sunk deep in his jaw and, the death of the animal resulting before they had been withdrawn, the muscles were now rigid and would not relax, so we had to saw off the paws of the bear to set the dog free."

The old timer was at first questioned about the validity of such a tale but with a manner showing half rage, half contempt, he informed his audience that the dog, a bitch, was buff-coloured. "Ah! but it was then we had the right dogs and not the straight and white pups of these days only good for barking and snarling."

Papier Éco-Logo™ / EcoLogo™ Paper

PRINTED IN CANADA